Stage Money

STAGE MONEY

The Business of the Professional Theater

Tim Donahue and Jim Patterson

The University of South Carolina Press

© 2010 University of South Carolina

Published by the University of South Carolina Press
Columbia, South Carolina 29208

www.sc.edu/uscpress

Manufactured in the United States of America

19 18 17 16 15 14 13 12 11 10   10 9 8 7 6 5 4 3 2 1

LIBRARY OF CONGRESS CATALOGING-IN-PUBLICATION DATA

Donahue, Tim, 1952–
    Stage money : the business of the professional theater / Tim Donahue
and Jim Patterson.
        p. cm.
    Includes bibliographical references and index.
    ISBN 978-1-57003-906-5 (cloth : alk. paper)—ISBN 978-1-57003-907-2
(pbk : alk. paper)
    1. Theater—United States—Finance. 2. Theater management—
United States. I. Patterson, Jim (Jim Aris) II. Title.
PN2293.E35.D66 2010
792.068′1—dc22   2009051100

This book was printed on Glatfelter Natures, a recycled paper
with 30 percent postconsumer content.

stage money (stâj mŭ´nĭ), *n., jargon.* Imitation money used in theatrical productions, in film, and by magicians

Contents

Illustrations

Preface

It's All about the Money

Oscar Wilde—a man of the theater and other places—defined a cynic as a man who knows the price of everything and the value of nothing. By that standard, *Stage Money* is a cynical book.

The value of the theater is art or at least entertainment. As an audience at the best theater, we see ourselves or others on stage in new or deeper ways and from psychological, social, or political perspectives, and we are moved to laughter and tears. Triumphant performances complete an aesthetic circle that leaves us welling up with contented excitement. Even through tears, that experience of completeness that the best art supplies is profoundly encouraging. Life has meaning for a few moments at least, and we can hope for humanity again.

None of the value of theater can be found here. This book is cynical, using Oscar Wilde's definition. We seek to give a bracing overview of the finances of the theater today. We want to know what the cost of theater is. These questions fascinate us:

How are theater performances organized financially today, meaning in the period between the 1999–2000 and 2007–2008 seasons?

From where does the money come and to where does it flow?

How do the finances of theater compare with those of other businesses?

How does the commercial theater compare with the not-for-profit theater?

To answer these and other questions, *Stage Money* presents models and approaches, some of which are new to the literature of the professional theater but will be recognized by anyone interested in other, more conventional businesses. In applying these models, we find ourselves often at odds with many of the traditional rules of thumb that abound in the professional theater.

For example, the common wisdom states that four of five commercial Broadway productions fail to recoup their initial investment; we demonstrate that this was not true in the years that are covered in this book. Common wisdom stresses that the risk of investing in the commercial theater is out of proportion to the potential for profit; we show that the risks were high but were probably commensurate with the average returns on investing in the commercial theater.

Common wisdom divides professional theater into Broadway and everything else. We provide a more contemporary division: between the commercial and the not-for-profit theater.

Common wisdom maintains that, by financial size and artistic purpose, the commercial and not-for-profit theaters are two very different activities. *Stage Money* demonstrates the new interreliance of these two parts of the American theater.

Stage Money makes sense of the mind-boggling array of prices for Broadway tickets by comparing the theater to the airlines, among other businesses, and describing the economic forces at work that make Broadway producers sell what is virtually the same seat for many different prices.

The authors of this book have fairly catholic tastes in theater. We like glitzy musicals, classic plays performed as classics and radical reimaginings of classic plays, the postmodern theater at least some of the time, family dramas, political theater, vaudeville, Brecht and Beckett at their best, shows in ninety-nine-seat black boxes and opera houses, pretty much all of it. We want *more* theater. We don't know how to get that, but we trust that a new perspective might open a wedge for new ideas on how to finance new and more theater.

We want the art and craft of theater, but some money must be behind the art somehow. The title, *Stage Money,* is a pun on the theater term for imitation money used in stage productions, but the money necessary to fund theater—both commercial and not-for-profit—is very *real* money indeed.

Theater has been slow to adopt fully many of the potent techniques of late-twentieth-century business—theater box offices didn't accept credit cards before 1979—but it is adopting many of them now. Older audience members can confirm that in many obvious ways the finances of the theater have changed. Some examples:

Once upon a time . . .	Today, for the most part . . .
A producer was a brand name and often something of a maverick: think "David Merrick."	There are often more producers listed above the title than actors on the stage.
Broadway producers originated and developed material through out-of-town tryouts.	Broadway producers cherry-pick the most interesting shows from not-for-profit regional theaters and from London.

Once upon a time . . .

A boffo hit, like the original production of *Oklahoma!*, ran for a record-setting 2,000 performances

Persons performing alone on stage were called "monologists" and often relegated to performing in ninety-nine-seat off-Broadway theaters or school auditoriums.

Ticket price was based on the location of your seat and day of the week

A polite letter to the box office, accompanied by a check and self-addressed stamped envelope would buy a ticket at no additional charge.

Broadway was filled almost solely by the work of commercial producers.

Only scalpers charged more than the highest list price of a Broadway ticket.

Today, for the most part . . .

The Phantom of the Opera played more than 9,200 performances as of January 2010, and it's still going. In all, twenty-six Broadway productions have played more than 2,000 performances.

Recent Broadway successes include these one-person shows: *The Year of Magical Thinking, Bridge & Tunnel,* and *Wishful Drinking.*

Price is often based on the demand for tickets and on the theatergoer's willingness to work to get a bargain.

If the shopper doesn't go to the box office, he or she can buy a ticket by phone or over the Internet and pay a substantial premium for the convenience.

Not-for-profit organizations make up a significant and growing portion of Broadway entertainment.

Producers of hit shows offer premium seats for up to three times the highest list price.

U.S. Expenditures on Theater

The U.S. Bureau of Economic Analysis estimates that about 4 percent of an American's personal consumption expenditures for recreation are spent on professional theater. This percentage has changed little since 1940. This is less than what is spent on magazines or newspapers, which garner about 6 percent each.

Of course, things have changed. Look at the main commercial street of your city. If you've lived in the same place for at least ten years, you've seen great changes in the businesses at street level. Some thrive; others fail. The failures open space for other entrepreneurs to pursue their ideas. To imagine one example: Starbucks opens on Main Street, and at first it seems the chain's effect on small businesses will be dire. In many cases, *surprise*, Starbucks draws to Main Street new customers who are flush enough to buy a four-dollar coffee once a day or several times a day. These new customers support existing businesses near the coffee store or will support the right new business when it opens. The area around Starbucks often flourishes. This is the ecology of Main Street. Later the Disney Corporation's entry to Broadway will be described. Like Starbucks on Main Street, Disney was feared by many on Broadway, but its presence has sparked new financial opportunities for other producers.

To take a larger perspective, few people imagined until recently that powerhouse corporations like General Motors or Sears would today be on the financial ropes, fighting for their lives. And Starbucks, used in the analogy about Main Street ecology above, was in difficult times in 2009.

This foment, a fight for survival between new and old businesses, describes more or less the ecology of Broadway, off-Broadway, the road, and of the not-for-profit theater. Elizabeth McCann, producer with others, of *Passing Strange, Well, The Goat or Who is Sylvia?*, and the recent revivals of *Equus, Who's Afraid of Virginia Woolf?*, and *Butley*, said of Broadway producing, "It's always been survival of the fittest and always will be."

Does America get the theater it deserves? We don't know, but we're certain America gets the theater it *pays* for.

This is a cynical conclusion, but other books can discuss and further the art of theater. This is *Stage Money*, a look at how theater is paid for.

But first some disclaimers are needed. In order to discuss financial and economic concepts, we present brief outlines of some very complex and interesting subjects. Look in other books for completeness and subtlety on these ideas. The selected bibliography cites some introductory texts.

Similarly we describe the legal structures of commercial and not-for-profit theater in a condensed outline. The general reader needs this background to understand who are the shareholders and stakeholders in professional theater. This is not a how-to book on theater producing. Several recent books cover this subject in varying amounts of detail and usefulness; see the bibliography.

The information in this book comes from public sources. By compiling the information in one place and structuring it through the lens of conventional business and investing, *Stage Money* provides an altered perspective on the business of theater. However, in many cases complete and validated data are unavailable, and the best figures that can be supplied are suggestive. More research is warranted.

A note on time frames: this book was written mostly in 2008 and early 2009. To allow time to know whether a given production was financially successful, we generally investigated shows that opened no later than the 2006–7 season. As a starting point, we arbitrarily chose the 1999–2000 season. Our blog with updated information on the business of theater can be found at http://www.stagemoney .net.

Acknowledgments

Thanks are owed to friends for reviewing early drafts of this book: Ken Cameron, freelance writer of fiction and nonfiction; Patti Gillespie, professor emeritus of the University of Maryland; Philip Hill, professor emeritus of Furman University; and Sara Nalley, professor of Columbia College, in Columbia, South Carolina. Any errors in this book, however, are solely the authors' responsibility.

The authors appreciate the support of the University of South Carolina Press and especially its assistant director for operations, Linda Haines Fogle. She was Jim Patterson's student some undisclosed number of years ago, and she did not hold that against him.

1

Commercial Theaters versus Not-for-Profit Theaters

Key Differences

When most people talk about American professional theater, the main division made is between Broadway and everything else. But really the division that better suits is the distinction between professional commercial theater and professional not-for-profit theater.

About one-quarter of new Broadway shows of late have been funded as not-for-profit. In the 2006–7 season, out of thirty-five show openings on Broadway, eight shows were not-for-profit. In the 2007–8 season, of thirty-seven productions, eleven were not-for-profit. Of the forty Broadway theaters, five are owned or leased and operated by not-for-profit entities. A sixth Broadway not-for-profit will be added if Second Stages makes good on its plan to purchase the Helen Hayes Theatre.

Except for Broadway, touring productions, and legitimate theater in Las Vegas, nearly all theater in the United States is not-for-profit. Two notable exceptions are a small number of dinner theaters, found mainly in the Midwest, and the African American touring play phenomenon most commonly called the "chitlin' circuit," discussed later. Dinner theaters cannot qualify as not-for-profit enterprises because they serve two unrelated purposes, presenting theater and serving up a nice piece of roast beef. The National Dinner Theatre Association has twenty-four members. Actors Equity reports the number of weeks worked in the dinner theater for its members have declined by 65 percent in the last twenty-five years. Currently dinner theater is continuing to decline in number and finances.

It would seem that once you say "commercial" and "not-for-profit," you've pretty much defined the difference between these two types of theater, but there are other differences that come directly from the main difference in financial goals. Some include:

Commercial Theater	Not-for-Profit Theater
Typically formed as a partnership or company to produce one play only and then disband.	Theoretically continues forever. Usually produces a slate of plays each season.
A production is often planned as an open-ended run, playing for as long as ticket sales support it.	A production is rarely planned as an open-ended run; not-for-profit theaters generally have closed runs, with established ending dates.
Producers do not necessarily own and operate the theater where the show is playing.	After the starting years, most groups own or lease long-term and maintain their own theater space.
Box office results determine if a show runs.	Only 40 to 60 percent of the budget comes from box office.
Profits for investors are taxable; losses are deductible for the most part.	Income in excess of costs is called "surplus" and is for maintained by the theater for another use. Donations to the not-for-profit theater are deductible for the most part.

The details of these differences are explored later.

It is a common mistake to gauge the vitality of the American professional theater solely or even primarily by Broadway. No one would judge American writing only by the best seller list, American movies solely by the week's top grossing film, or music merely by the groups that can fill a football stadium. Similarly theater is not described by its commercial operations alone.

We are convinced that the heart of American theater is the not-for-profit theater. Commercial theater gets the greatest attention in the popular press because of the size of its budgets, the concentration of activity on Broadway and environs, and the availability of the national media headquartered in Manhattan. By contrast the impact of any one not-for-profit theater is usually felt within a single community. Since theater is distinguished by being a live event, no other media can duplicate the aesthetic experience of theater. Thus, for many people, the not-for-profit theater is their main access to the theater experience.

Though it was once primarily a place where musicals and boulevard comedies went after they left Broadway, the not-for-profit theater is increasingly an important cultural engine developing new plays and musicals. It is the rare successful

Broadway show that originates on Broadway. We looked at the origins of Broadway openings in the 2006–7 and 2007–8 seasons as examples. Of thirty-three openings in 2007, sixteen originated in the not-for-profit theater, and seven were imported from abroad. New Broadway productions in 2008 totaled thirty-two, of which nineteen were from not-for-profit theaters and five were from abroad.

In 2006–7, of fourteen shows that *Variety,* the primary trade journal of the entertainment industry, labeled flops, six originated on Broadway. Of eight shows labeled as hits, two originated on Broadway. Not-for-profit sources of hit shows included the La Jolla Playhouse, San Diego; Alliance Theatre, Atlanta; and Center Theatre Group, Los Angeles.

The Tony Awards for 2004 were a minisweep for the not-for-profit theater: best musical, best play, best revival of a musical, and best revival of a play all went to not-for-profit theaters or shows that originated in not-for-profit theaters. Between 1999–2000 and 2007–8, 61 percent of the "Best . . ." Tony Awards went to not-for-profit productions or not-for-profit originated productions, and 17 percent went to productions originating abroad. Fewer than one-quarter of these superlative kudos—22 percent—went to shows originating on Broadway.

What Is a Broadway Theater?

In the popular imagination, Broadway is any commercial live theater in New York City. Actually Broadway defines only theaters in midtown Manhattan that seat at least five hundred. Only productions in these theaters are eligible for Tony Awards. Union rules are different for Broadway houses than for other New York professional venues. The number of Broadway houses varies as theaters are built or remodeled or turned to other uses. In 2009 there were forty Broadway theaters, seventeen owned by the Shubert Organization, six by Jujamcyn Theatres, and nine by the Nederlander Organization. Four are owned or controlled by not-for-profit theaters. Of the remaining four, one is owned by Key Brands Entertainment, one leased long-term from the City of New York by the Disney Corporation, and two are independent: the Helen Hayes Theatre, owned by the New York Times Company, and Circle in the Square, a small house built in the underground spaces of Paramount Plaza. Circle was a not-for-profit theater that went bankrupt in 1996; now its facility is a commercial theater.

A not-for-profit theater, Second Stages, is planning to purchase the Helen Hayes and begin presenting there in 2010; this will bring the number of not-for-profit Broadway theaters to six. The Helen Hayes is the smallest Broadway house with 597 seats, built in 1912. The largest at 1,933 seats is the Gershwin Theatre, opened in 1972.

The Two Sides of Professional Theater—
Commercial and Not-for-Profit

The scope, ambition, and prizewinning accomplishment of the largest not-for-profit theaters in the United States are truly astonishing. By contrast the commercial theater relies on long-running musicals, which make large profits. Broadway commercial producers have largely abandoned the serious new play and the small musical to the not-for-profit. And, in much of the United States, the main professional theater available to audiences comes from not-for-profit organizations. For all these reasons, the most important division in the professional theater today is between the commercial and the not-for-profit theaters.

Intermission

Disney on Broadway

For all the glamour of Broadway, it has always been in some ways a mom-and-pop business. For many years commercial Broadway theaters were owned by only three companies. Broadway producers were a small handful of people, mostly men. Newcomers often lost their shirts, so the number of people involved as a continuing community was small. Then came Mickey Mouse.

No one knows how much money Disney makes on Broadway. As a corporation Disney doesn't report profit and loss for a single line of business. Disney Theatrical Productions is just one part of the Disney Corporation's Studio Entertainment group, a division that grossed $7.5 billion in 2006.

Some commentators have speculated, surprisingly, that Disney is not focused on profit on Broadway. Rather it seeks to establish products that can be sold all over the world, in live productions, ice shows, and toys and other hard goods while stoking Disney's existing DVD, television, and theme-park businesses. This process is known as "vertical integration," defined as ownership by one organization of more than one stage of a product life cycle.

Disney entered the commercial live theater in 1992 with two simultaneous efforts, a stage production based on its animated film *Beauty and the Beast* and the rebuilding of the New Amsterdam Theatre on 42nd Street. The traditional Broadway community worried. Disney seemed to have endless financial capability and the clout of an international marketing organization. Feelings on Broadway were further inflamed when the gift shop for *Beauty and the Beast* sold almost ten thousand dollars' worth of souvenirs at the first preview performance.

Broadway veterans were also concerned about New York City's financial support for the remodeling of the New Amsterdam Theatre. The city gave Disney a $21 million low-interest loan for the renovation, while Disney put up $8 million, and the city gave Disney a 99-year lease at a token rent.

Beauty and the Beast proved that the Broadway traditionalists were right, at least about aesthetics. The stage musical was seen by reviewers as stodgy and overly literal, resembling a Disney theme-park show. The reviews didn't matter to audiences, who came in droves with their children and helped change the face of Broadway. When the show closed in July 2007, it had played 5,464 performances—the sixth longest-running musical to that date—and grossed more than $429 million in New York alone.

Disney's commitment to rebuild the New Amsterdam was an important element in the city's effort to change 42nd Street from a drink-and-drug-and-sex blighted couple of blocks to a name-brand, spanking new, and inviting urban theme park. It must be said that some folks are nostalgic for the old 42nd Street, but, considered in terms of making money, the revamped 42nd Street is an undeniable success.

It didn't hurt that the first show in the remodeled New Amsterdam was Disney's staging of its animated movie *The Lion King.* Perhaps having learned from the critical reception of *Beauty,* Disney picked one of the not-for-profit theater's most visually inventive directors, Julie Taymor, for *The Lion King* and came up with a show that wowed critics and audiences alike.

Disney's Alan Levey, who has been general manager of three Disney Broadway shows, explains the impact of *The Lion King* this way:

> *The Lion King* would have remained an animated film released in 1994, to be re-released ten years later in video, and in the interim, it would have remained dormant. Along comes a Broadway musical that opens in 1997, three years after the film opened, and suddenly, there is a reiteration and reinvigoration of *The Lion King.* While a successful stage production's profitability may not meet that of a successful film over the course of the film's theatrical, video, and DVD releases on a dollar-for-dollar basis—although all productions of *The Lion King* internationally are certainly profitable—it does extend the life of, and add equity to, a property significantly. And it generates additional opportunities for merchandising and positive press that otherwise wouldn't exist.

Others maintain that of course Disney is making money on Broadway. In the summer of 2007, a full-price ticket for Disneyworld was $71; a full price orchestra seat at the Minskoff Theatre for Disney's *The Lion King* was $121.25.

Thomas Schumacher, president of Disney Theatricals, summed up the financial impact of Disney's *Aida:* "It recouped and made a lot of money. Now a show like *Aida* around the world, this year, next year, with no performances in New York, will make $5 million a year. In foreign productions and high school productions, second-class productions, and amateur productions. So that fuels the ongoing nature of what we've been doing."

As of the end of 2007, Disney Theatrical Productions had thirteen international productions of *Beauty and the Beast, The Lion King,* Elton John and Tim Rice's *Aida, Mary Poppins* (a coproduction by Disney and Cameron Mackintosh), and *The Little Mermaid. Beauty and the Beast* had been seen in 14 countries. As of October 2009, *The Lion King* had grossed more than $3.6 billion on stage and had been seen by more than 50 million people worldwide.

In the pipeline at various times and in various stages of development have been or are a new version of *Pinocchio,* a musical based on the Harlem Globetrotters, a touring revue of songs from the Disney collection, and probably other productions as well. Some have likened Disney Theatrical to the old Hollywood studios, which would have a number of films in various stages of development at any one time, but now Disney is taking that assembly-line approach to developing live theater.

Meanwhile it seems that Broadway has not been hurt by Disney's entry. Instead Broadway has rediscovered the family audience for musicals, which it has satisfied with financially successful shows such as *Wicked* and to a lesser extent *Legally Blonde,* which are particularly appealing to teenage and preteenage girls. The Broadway League's audience study for the 2007–8 season found the highest percentage of children and teenagers attending Broadway theater in the past thirty years: 12.4 percent.

2

●●

Commercial Theater On- and Off-Broadway

Financial and Legal Structures

The legal and financial shape of commercial theater production evolves over time in response to changes in law, tax rules, and the availability of capital. It always has. Theater people are creative, and not only on stage.

In 1599 the landlord of Shakespeare's performing group, the Lord Chamberlain's Men, would not renew its lease. So the acting troupe dismantled the theater building in a matter of days around Christmas time, moved the timber and wood across the river outside of the city of London, and used that material to construct the Globe Theater. The Globe was built in an area called Southwark, known for bear-baiting pits, prostitution, and pickpockets. Sounds a little bit like the old 42nd Street! And we know about it in detail because its relocation was followed by years of lawsuits, which makes this four-hundred-year-old story sound even more modern. This historical anecdote is offered as evidence that theater people adapted in the face of adversity and challenge in the late sixteenth century, as they still do in our day.

The most common form and shape for a commercial theater production is described here, though the overview glosses over a lot of details. Any specific production will alter some or all of this structure, depending on where the negotiating power lies among the producers, investors, authors, designers, and performers.

It must be said that not only negotiating power shapes the financial structure of commercial theater; tradition also plays a big role. Because each producing entity is staging only one play, producers have been leery of risking that one show on a financial innovation.

The dominant legal form for large businesses in the United States is the corporation. The concept of incorporation goes back centuries, but its modern form in business took hold in the twentieth century. A corporation is a kind of artificial person. A corporation can sue and be sued, own assets in its own name, sign contracts, offer shares to investors that can be sold without affecting the corporation's legal identity, and continue despite a shareholder's death or withdrawal. Furthermore a corporation's investors have limited liability. This last characteristic is very important. Shareholders can lose only the value of their shares if the corporation defaults on debt, is sued, or is found guilty of criminal acts. The shareholders' other wealth is safe from the corporation's losses.

For reasons that will be explained elsewhere in *Stage Money*, not-for-profit theaters are corporations, but new commercial theater productions are seldom mounted by corporations—Disney excepted, of course.

Producer and Investors

Until the mid 1990s, the common form for a Broadway production was a limited liability partnership. There was one general partner—called the producer—and multiple limited partners, called investors and sometimes called "angels." The limited partners put up all the money for the show and had no say in any decisions about the show, financial or artistic. This producer-investor relationship has been traditional, but good management and financial reasons remain for it to continue.

The general partner can legally put up money but usually doesn't. Remember the lines from the Mel Brooks Broadway musical *The Producers:* "There are two rules for being a producer. Rule one: Never. Use. Your. Own. Money! What is the second rule? NEVER USE YOUR OWN MONEY!!!"

The general partner, or the producer, makes all decisions about the production and splits profits after recoupment with the limited partners, or the investors, fifty-fifty. In addition producers receive some percent of weekly gross sales whether the show is profitable or not and a weekly fee described as "office expenses." A potential investor should know that a producer can make money on a show even if the investors do not.

The producer is entitled to that big share of the profits for many reasons. He or she is knowledgeable about the business end of theatrical production and has discovered or commissioned the material and risked money doing so. The producer also has made legal filings to create the partnership and has produced backers' auditions to entice the limited partners to invest. A producer has usually invested time and money on other shows that for one reason or another never materialized. And although most of the producer's expenditures prior to attracting investors are repaid from the production budget, by law the producer cannot be reimbursed for expenses related to attracting investors, such as the cost of backers' auditions.

The producer has relationships with theater owners, creative people such as directors and designers, marketing staff with expertise in the theater, builders of scenery and costumes, and so on. The producer knows how to select and organize all these companies and individuals to make a show happen.

The Producer's Real Percentage of Profit

Today the producer usually gives away in negotiations some of his share of profits to attract investors, star actors, and directors, and so on. It's not unusual for the producer who starts with 50 percent to end up with 13 to 15 percent of the profits, in addition to weekly payments for so-called office expenses and some percentage of the box office gross.

Don't cry for the producer; recall that he or she can make money even if the investors do not. Consider as one example the musical *Wicked:* in January 2009, after running five-and-a-half years, *Wicked* was grossing about $1.3 million per week on Broadway. The producers were sharing 2 to 3 percent of the gross revenues, or between $26,000 and $39,000 per week. This is before their share of the show's profit, and *Wicked* is profitable; the show recouped its initial investment of about $14 million in 14 months. In addition there were road companies of *Wicked* in Chicago, Los Angeles, and Louisville that together grossed more than $6 million in the first full week of January 2009, during which *Wicked* posted house record grosses in both Los Angeles and Louisville. From the road shows, the producers receive their percent of gross revenues, weekly office expenses, and a share of profit. *Wicked* was playing in London, Stuttgart, Melbourne, and Tokyo too.

Most important, the producer takes almost all the risk associated with the production. The limited partners' only risk is the loss of their investment; that's why they're labeled *limited.* The general partner—the producer—is personally responsible for losses in excess of the investment. It's hard to imagine losses in excess of the investment in a well-managed production, except perhaps for an injury for which the production wasn't adequately insured or a legal fiasco such as a libel or copyright infringement suit.

The limited partners have no say in the running of the show. If they did, they would no longer be considered by the courts as limited partners and thus would be potentially liable for losses in excess of their investments.

Why Not a Corporation?

There is no legal reason a Broadway production can't be incorporated. In a corporation only the corporation's assets are at risk. The problem is that a corporation is taxed on its earnings *and* the shareholders are taxed on dividends the corporation pays; earnings are taxed twice. Additionally corporations cannot quickly move losses to investors. If Broadway angels suffer losses, at least they want to take the losses off their taxes quickly.

Corporations in other kinds of entertainment, mostly motion pictures, have produced Broadway shows as part of a portfolio of entertainment investments. The Disney Corporation has been notably successful on Broadway. But as "Intermission: Disney on Broadway" points out, Disney is not solely interested in the profit of one Broadway production. And the drawback of double taxation does not figure in Disney's decisions.

Before Disney, corporations including ABC, Universal Studios, Miramax Films, Fox Searchlight, and Suntory Whiskey (a Japanese distiller) have occasionally participated as limited investors in theatrical productions. For instance, in 1956, CBS Records invested in *My Fair Lady* so that it could produce the cast album for the show. With the show's profitable run, the movie sale, and the cast album, CBS Records made money across the board. Since Disney's entry other film studio corporations have looked to move properties to Broadway. Few so far have had the success that Disney has had on Broadway. For example, Warner Brothers Theatre Ventures had a particularly disastrous experience with the 2006 musical *Lestat,* based on the Anne Rice vampire novels and films. It ran for thirty-nine performances with an estimated loss of $12 million.

Commercial theatrical partnerships produce just a single property because there is a specific time when they dissolve the business. Without a date for dissolution, the IRS will consider the business a corporation no matter what it calls itself. Traditionally, Broadway partnerships last eighteen years.

With New York State's Limited Liability Law of 1994, commercial productions could form limited liability companies and such companies have now become the dominant legal form for commercial theater. The main difference between the companies and limited liability partnerships is that with a limited liability company, no one is personally liable for losses in excess of the company's assets. Instead of general partners, the principals are called "managing members." Managing members may or may not have authority over the company's decisions; the nature of a managing member's authority and responsibility is laid out in the legal papers that create the company.

More Producers than Actors

Nowadays, it's not unusual for a commercial production of a play to have more producers' names above the title than there are actors on the stage. Gone are the days of David Merrick, the legendary, daring, and cantankerous Broadway producer of such hits as *Hello, Dolly!, Gypsy,* and *42nd Street,* along with dozens of important straight, that is to say, nonmusical, plays, many imported from London. Merrick was the self-crowned king of his productions. One season in the 1960s he produced a half-dozen plays and musicals, once opening four in a month. He frequently won multiple Tony Awards in the same season.

Merrick was known for his love of publicity stunts. One of his most famous was for the 1961 musical *Subways Are for Sleeping.* Merrick found seven New Yorkers who had the same names as New York's theater critics. Merrick invited them to the musical and got permission to use their names and pictures in an ad with quotes such as "One of the few great musical comedies of the last thirty years" and "A fabulous musical. I love it." Only one newspaper published the ad, but publicity from the gag helped the otherwise forgettable musical remain open for six months.

It is said that Merrick was so sure that *42nd Street* would be a hit that he refused to open the Broadway production until each investor he'd previously convinced to invest in the show had sold his share back to Merrick. Such independence and bullying are now gone from Broadway.

Because budgets are now so large—producing a nonmusical play on Broadway can easily require an investment of $2 million and musicals upward of $10 million —producers find it more prudent to back a portion of many productions rather than just one or two big productions a season. It's roughly comparable to the Wall Street investor diversifying a portfolio. When a show flops, an individual producer licks his or her wounds for that one but maintains the hope that another show will be a hit.

Producer Richard Frankel said, "Those old shows used to open and recoup in six or seven months. If they lost money, they lost a relatively modest amount of money. These things [today's Broadway shows] can sink you. If you try to do them yourself, they can be career ending." In 2005 Jed Bernstein, then president of what is now called the Broadway League (the League of Theatre Owners and Producers before the end of 2007), said, "The skill set that a producer needs in current Broadway environment has changed dramatically over the decades." Bernstein cited a number of changes including "the dramatic rise in financial and development importance of the road [touring productions outside of Broadway], the increase in the number and complexity of marketing channels, and the sheer number of people involved on the both the management and creative side."

Why does it require at least $10 million to open a Broadway musical? Producer Tom Viertel has the answer: "Here's how it goes. Three-and-a-half million dollars for the physical production. A million to two million dollars to put the physical production into the theatre and conduct previews and work calls during the period when you're getting the show right. A million to a million-and-a-half dollars in advertising. Two million dollars for an out-of-town [tryout] which you might mitigate with income from the out-of-town. And the balance is in rehearsal costs and administrative costs and creative fees and stuff like that. Those are the big things."

What role all these producers play in the management of the production depends on the written agreement among the parties. In many cases the associate producers with names above the title are supplying a significant portion of the investment only and have no say in the management. In other cases duties are divided or decisions are made by consensus. Usually the agreement will specify that if consensus can't be reached, one producer breaks the tie and makes the decision. In a theatrical production, things can't stop for arbitration.

Some followers of the Broadway theater believe that the demise of the individual producer has led to a certain lack of vision, a committee-shaped blandness and sameness, in the current Broadway work. On the other hand, there are commentators who contend the reduced leadership from a single producer has led to the rising influence of directors.

For clarity we will treat the producer as always being one person when discussing the producer's responsibilities and profit share.

The Option

The option is an agreement between the producer and the owner of the rights to the work being produced. The rights owner receives a payment in return for an exclusive commitment that the producer may stage the work if the production opens in some limited period, typically six months. The option specifies that the producer can renew it for additional periods in exchange for more option payments. If no production is staged in this period, all rights revert to the rights owner, who keeps the options payments and can seek options from other producers. The producer's option allows the production of the optioned material on Broadway, off-Broadway, or in some other first-class production. *First-class production* specifies a show which has

- a first-class cast, meaning that the performers are members of Actors Equity Association (Equity);
- a first-class director, meaning that the director is a member of Equity or the Stage Directors and Choreographers Society (SDC); and
- a venue that is a first-class theater. Equity maintains a list of first-class theaters nationwide. In brief they are places where shows have extended or open-ended runs, not venues that house one-night-stands.

Productions that are not first-class typically do not get an option but instead obtain a limited *license* to produce a play. A license allows mounting the play in a given locale for a given duration but doesn't include the gamut of additional rights that an option does.

The optioned material may be an unproduced script, a script the producer has seen in London or at a not-for-profit theater, or an older script ripe for revival. In the case of some musicals, a play, novel, short story, or movie is optioned, and the producer recruits a composer, lyricist, and book writer to adapt it for the musical stage. In all these cases there will be one or more options required before the producer can begin to create a production. For purposes of discussion, this section assumes the simplest case: optioning an existing original script for a play.

Based on the specifics of the option agreement, the playwright may have veto authority on the hiring of other major creative people such as the director and designers. The playwright may attend any or all rehearsals and gets reimbursed for travel to do so. During any run the playwright may purchase a number of *house seats,* typically six each night. If the playwright doesn't buy them or let friends and relatives buy them, the house seats are released for general sale 48 hours before curtain. *House seats* are choice, well-located seats that the theater owner and producer are obliged to keep available for certain qualified people to buy. Unbought house seats are released to the public on various schedules, determined by the specific contract. Most important, the playwright receives a royalty payment from weekly gross ticket sales, typically 5 percent until the investment is recouped and 10 percent after recoupment. Usually the producer, as a result of fulfilling his option for a first-class production, can also organize touring versions and foreign productions.

Subsidiary Rights

In addition the producer shares in subsidiary rights if the first-class production runs long enough. Of course, if it doesn't run long enough, the subsidiary rights probably are of little value. The theory supporting this sharing is that the producer, by taking the significant monetary risks of mounting a successful production of the play, increases the value of the play and so deserves a share of the subsidiary profits.

Subsidiary rights include a share in the author's receipts from film, television, and other stage productions, although generally amateur production royalties are excluded. The subsidiary rights differ based on the specifics of the option contract, but it is not unusual for the producer to receive 50 percent of the author's profits from productions in other media, 50 percent of stock theater productions for five years, with 25 percent for the next three years after that, and 20 percent of revivals staged in the next forty years. Commercial products, such as dolls, clothing, and so on, are also included in typical subsidiary rights agreements. Investors in the original production usually receive a 50 percent share of the producers' income from subsidiary rights, through the end of the original partnership that created the entitlement to the subsidiary rights. The common length of the first-class partnership is eighteen years.

Income from subsidiary rights can be significant. After forty-two years of returns for an investment in the original off-Broadway production of *The Fantasticks* and after the show finally closed, at least one investor reported receiving a check for his share of subsidiary rights for *The Fantasticks* that was more than his original investment.

Producer Jim Freydberg has said, "Broadway isn't where you make the money anymore. It's where you establish the project so you can make the money. When you mount a show now, you really have to think about where it's going to play later." Freydberg's is an extreme point of view, but it emphasizes the importance of subsidiary rights to the value of an option.

General Manager

After identifying a potential production and obtaining an option, the producer hires a general manager. A general manager negotiates contracts and administers and supervises financial procedures, including banking, preparing budgets, paying bills, supervising ticket sales, and producing the weekly profit/loss statement. The general manager is often the liaison between artistic personnel and producer. As one commentator noted, the general manager does whatever the producer doesn't want to do. In some cases a producer and the producer's staff will also hire out as general manager for shows they do not produce.

The general manager is usually the first hire because it is the general manager who drafts a budget for the production. The investment agreements must by law specify budget amounts. Up to opening, the general manager serves much of the role of a *project manager* in a nontheatrical business. Budgeting is an art. Roger Alan Gindi, president of Gindi Theatrical Management, remembers, "On *Oleanna,* . . . I budgeted about $100 thousand in reserve for preview and operating losses. However, the initial demand for tickets was so high that we started to make an operating profit from the first performance. . . . Other shows have not been so lucky and have had to take priority loans to keep the show running, despite a generous reserve in the capitalization."

The general manager also takes some responsibility for organizing investor auditions, also known as *backers' auditions,* if any are held. Backers' auditions are typically fifty–sixty minutes, not the full script. And they're expensive. Director fees alone for backers' auditions are typically $1,500 to $2,500. Multiple backers' auditions may be necessary to raise the investment. The extreme case, as it is with so many things in the commercial theater, is *The Fantasticks*. First produced off-Broadway in 1960 for a budget of $16,500, *The Fantasticks* required twenty-seven backers' auditions.

The general manager remains with the show during the run and usually assumes the same duties for any road companies spawned by the New York production. The knowledge the general manager brings to a production, the ability to lead a team and negotiate among the members of that team, and the knowledge of a particular show when it comes time to organize a road company are invaluable to the success of a production.

Theater License

The producer must find an available theater appropriate for the optioned play and negotiate a license agreement with the theater owner. The agreement between the production and the theater owner is called a license—not a lease—because neither side wants to expose the agreement to the extensive requirements and vagaries of landlord/tenant law.

Theaters receive a weekly minimum payment against a percentage of gross receipts. Because the theater owner's remuneration depends on the box office, in busy times the producer may have to woo the theater owner, making a convincing case that the the play is strong and has box office potential.

If the gross receipts fall below a contractually set amount for one or two weeks, either the theater owner or the producer may terminate the contract using a license provision called the *stop clause*. Termination of the contract will require the show to move to another theater or, more likely, to close.

The theater maintains the money for ticket sales for future performances in an escrow account until the respective performances occur. The argument is that, should a show suddenly close, the producer may not have sufficient assets from which to repay ticket holders for future performances. The theater owner always has the physical asset of the theater itself to protect. How interest earned from future sales accounts is shared between the theater owner and the production is detailed in the license agreement.

For the license payment, the theater is a four-wall rental, taken "as is." No lighting equipment, sound equipment, or draperies are included, except for the main curtain, known as the *house drape*. In fact the producer pays a charge for any day when air conditioning is used in the theater. The theater provides box office staff, ushers, heating, and normal maintenance and cleaning. By tradition some employees are hired by the theater owner although their salaries are passed through to the producer, and everything else is the producer's responsibility.

The producer agrees that the production will stay in the theater for the run of the play; that other productions of the same play will not be mounted nearby; that sets, props, and costumes will be fireproofed; that the production will carry insurance; and other particulars. The agreement between the theater and producer specifies how income from concessions and souvenirs is split.

During the run the theater is entitled to buy a certain number of house seats to each performance, determined by the agreement. When the show closes, the producer must remove property within a limited time frame, typically forty-eight hours but sometimes as few as six.

Director, Designers, Actors, and Others

All the other players in commercial theater are represented by unions, which set minimum contract standards for their members. For Broadway productions the unions negotiate contracts with the Broadway League. Broadway producers who are not members of the league, such as the Disney corporation, negotiate separate agreements.

Although playwrights and composers for the theater typically belong to the Dramatists Guild, a trade group, the Dramatists Guild cannot act as a union for these individuals. Playwrights and composers are not employees under legal definition and so cannot at present be represented by a union. The guild publishes approved contracts, but they are not minimum contracts negotiated between the guild and the league and so are not binding on any of the parties.

Minimum fees and royalties for theater artists are just that: minimum. Depending on the perceived value a creative individual can add to a production, he or she can negotiate anything producers and their investors will agree to. Actors do not get royalties under the union agreement, but some star actors negotiate a share of either gross receipts or profit. Designers are not required to get royalties under the union agreements, but some designers negotiate a percentage of box office grosses. Negotiated percentages of the profits generally come out of the producer's 50 percent share of profits.

Union contracts specify things other than salaries and fringe benefits. The Actors Equity Association agreement with the Broadway League is more than 175 pages long, describing audition procedures, work conditions, travel reimbursement, sick leave, replacing an actor, payment for videotaping the show, and on and on.

In addition to Equity, which represents actors and stage managers, there are two main unions. Directors and choreographers are represented by the Stage Directors and Choreographers Society (SDC), which was named the Society of Stage Directors and Choreographers or SSDC until May 2009. United Scenic Artists, International Alliance of Theatrical Stage Employees (IATSE) Local 829, is for set, costume, and lighting designers.

Additional theatrical unions include mostly other locals of IATSE:

- the Theatrical Protective Union, IATSE Local 1, which represents in New York City the carpenters, electricians, house crews, and any people used to load and unload scenery and electrics, and sound designers;
- the Treasurers and Ticket Sellers Union, IATSE Local 751;
- IATSE Local 306, Motion Picture Projectionists, Operators, Video Technicians, Theatre Employees, and Allied Crafts representing ushers, ticket takers, and doormen;
- International Union of Operating Engineers, Local 30, for heating and air conditioning service in theaters;
- Theatrical Wardrobe Attendants Union, IATSE Local 764;
- Make-Up Artists and Hair Stylists Union, IATSE Local 798; and
- Association of Theatrical Press Agents and Managers, IATSE Local 18032.

Two additional unions are not locals of IATSE:

• Service Employees International Union, Local 32BJ for custodians, and so on;
• Associated Musicians of Greater New York, American Federation of Musicians Local 802.

In all, at least a dozen unions are involved in creating and maintaining a Broadway production.

Off-Broadway Commercial Productions

The off-Broadway commercial production is very much like the Broadway version although the dollar amounts are smaller. The profit potential is smaller as well. Off-Broadway theaters must have fewer than five hundred seats. Off-Broadway audiences expect to pay a lower ticket price than they would for Broadway shows. All these upside limits on revenue mean that off-Broadway productions can afford only limited advertising.

Producer Marc Routh said, "One of the challenges that we have as producers is to let people know about our shows: and especially off-Broadway, we have limited dollars. A Broadway show will spend $75,000, $100,000 a week to advertise. Off-Broadway, we spend between $6,000 and $20,000 a week to advertise. And I think there aren't a lot of shows that can afford to spend $20,000 a week."

In addition to having fewer union "feather-bedding" rules than Broadway, off-Broadway union minimums are lower. Figure 2.1 presents some union minimums as of 2008. We've chosen minimums for a straight play, single set, limited number of characters.

Union minimums for off-Broadway are less than those for Broadway productions. Compare the gross finances for two straight plays, one off-Broadway and one on. When the off-Broadway production of Tracy Letts's thriller *Bug* closed in February 2006 after an eleven-month run that sold about $2 million in tickets, it essentially broke even, just paying back the investors. Subsidiary rights, including the movie sale, certainly give the investors some profit. The production cost $200,000 to mount and about $34,000 per week to run. Contrast this off-Broadway production with a Broadway straight play, the Kevin Spacey-starring revival of *A Moon for the Misbegotten*, which cost $2 million to mount and about $50,000 per week to run until recoupment. Of that nut Spacey got $10,000 per week, which jumped to $30,000 per week after recoupment. *Moon for the Misbegotten* paid back its investors and gave them a 30 percent profit. Off-Broadway is cheaper than Broadway, but the lower cost doesn't always result in profit for investors.

Sophisticated producers consider whether a Broadway or off-Broadway production is the financial way to go with a particular property. For the June 2005 star-cast revival of David Rabe's *Hurlyburly,* the producers were widely experienced; Jeffrey B. Seller and Kevin McCollum had mounted shows on Broadway before,

Director (dramatic productions)

Broadway	Off-Broadway
$19,020 fee	$8,866 fee, if 400+ seats
Plus 3.5% of operating profit;	*Plus* $5,964 advance against
minimum of $840 weekly	2% of operating profit

Set Designer (single set)

Broadway	Off-Broadway
$7,635 fee	$2,005 to $6,031 depending
Plus $1,914 advance against	on theater size
$275 weekly payment	*Plus* $84 to $162 weekly payment

Lighting Designer (single set)

Broadway	Off-Broadway
$5,725 fee	$1,957 to $4,061 depending
Plus $1,436 advance against	on theater size
$275 weekly payment	*Plus* $84 to $162 weekly payment

Costume Designer (1–7 characters)

Broadway	Off-Broadway
$5,581 fee	$2,005 to $6,031 for 1–9
Plus $1,177 advance against	characters
$275 weekly payment	*Plus* $84 to $162 weekly payment

Actors

Broadway	Off-Broadway
$1,509 weekly	$497 to $872 depending
	on theater size

Fig. 2.1 Some union minimums on- and off-Broadway as of 2008

including *Rent, Avenue Q,* and Baz Luhrman's commercial production of the Puccini opera *La Boheme.* They chose to put *Hurlyburly* in an off-Broadway house. Seller told the *New York Times,* "If you go to Broadway, you will spend a minimum of $2 million before the play is seen by a single audience member. We think the bill is too high." This off-Broadway *Hurlyburly* cost $650,000 to mount; it had a weekly operating budget of $95,000, which the producers maintain was less than half the weekly operating budget for a Broadway production.

Producers come to the opposite conclusion as well, rejecting off-Broadway for the bigger potential profit of Broadway. *Avenue Q* is an adult musical with puppets who sing songs titled "The Internet Is for Porn" and "Everyone's a Little Bit Racist."

The show was a hit in the 125-seat Vineyard Theatre in 2003 and was going to move to a larger house. Many thought the material was far from Broadway fare. Still, one producer speaking for the team of *Avenue Q* producers, Kevin McCollum, said the financial numbers made the production viable only on Broadway. The show has a cast of seven, plus six understudies and an orchestra of at least four—six on Broadway. "With 19 company members, you're not an Off Broadway show," McCollum said. At the very least, McCollum added, they would need 499 seats—the size of only the two largest off-Broadway houses—and those theaters were booked. The off-Broadway not-for-profit production of *Avenue Q*, created by two not-for-profit theaters, the Vineyard and the New Group, along with enhancement money from interested commercial producers, cost $475,000 to mount. The Broadway production was estimated to cost $3 million to mount. The producer's judgment paid off. *Avenue Q* closed on Broadway in September 2009, after grossing over $141 million. Given the producer's analysis quoted above, it is ironic that the production

Producers Compared to High-End Art Gallery Owners

It's interesting to compare the split between the producer and the investors to the split between an artist and a gallery owner, typically 50 percent of the sale price of an artwork. At first consideration that split seems to shortchange the artist. For his or her share, the artist puts up creativity, sweat, and emotional lifeblood. By comparison the gallery owner puts up rent, lights, publicity, advertising, and wine and cheese for the opening. The gallery owner courts a circle of interested collectors and knows how to close a sale in a sophisticated way. This contribution can potentially increase the value of the artist's work. An important gallery owner has a reputation that influences collectors and museums, and showing an artist's work in such a gallery legitimizes the artist.

For an example of this potential influence and its financial impact, consider Leo Castelli, one of the most successful art dealers of the twentieth century. Castelli was instrumental in establishing the artistic and commercial standings of many artists, including Robert Rauschenberg, Jasper Johns, Frank Stella, James Rosenquist, Roy Lichtenstein, Andy Warhol, and many more.

What the gallery owner brings to the relationship are things that most artists are by temperament and experience unable or unwilling to add. Similarly the producer brings to the commercial theater partnership experience and knowledge that the investors do not have. A successful first production adds value to a playscript in a way analogous to how an exhibit in a major gallery can increase the value of an artist's work.

then moved to a large off-Broadway house to extend its New York run. No Broadway show in memory has been transferred to Off-Broadway.

The Size of Commercial Off-Broadway

One can only estimate the number of commercial theaters off-Broadway. The League of Off-Broadway Theatre Owners and Producers (LOOBTOP), founded in 1959 to foster theatrical productions produced in off-Broadway theaters, has nine member theaters. LOOBTOP lists another seventeen commercial theaters that are not members of the league; it makes no claim to having a complete list. Thus there are at least twenty-six commercial off-Broadway spaces compared with thirty-five commercial Broadway houses.

Recent years have seen a lot of change in the available commercial performance spaces off-Broadway. In calendar 2006, at least six off-Broadway venues closed, to be replaced with condominiums, a church, the studio of a Christian TV network, and a Sephora cosmetics boutique. Included in this list were such venerable marquee names as the Promenade Theatre, the John Houseman Theatre, the Douglas Fairbanks Theatre, and the Variety Arts. On the other hand, New World Stages opened five new.theater spaces in 2004; 37 Arts opened three in 2005; and the Snapple Theatre Center opened two theaters in the same year.

We gathered information on off-Broadway openings for the 2004–5 and 2005–6 seasons. Each season saw a few more than 130 productions. About one-quarter of these were commercial productions; the rest were not-for-profit. Revival or classical plays made up just over 20 percent of off-Broadway productions. Two or three shows transferred to Broadway each season; one show each season transferred to a different, often larger, off-Broadway house.

The average run of all off-Broadway shows in 2004–5 was 9.6 weeks. For most productions, with eight outings a week, this amounts to an average of 76 performances. For 2005–6 the average was 6.2 weeks, or about 49 performances. By comparison the average run on Broadway in the period from 1999–2000 through 2005–6 was 290 performances, or approximately 36 calendar weeks.

Commercial productions off-Broadway run a little longer than not-for-profit productions. In the 2005–6 season the average commercial off-Broadway run was 7.7 weeks. In the 2004–5 season the average commercial off-Broadway run was 17.2 weeks, significantly more than the not-for-profit average. Note that 2005 saw the premiere of *Altar Boyz,* a hit off-Broadway musical that was still running as 2009 began. If *Altar Boyz* is removed from the statistics, the commercial productions in 2005–6 averaged 12.6 weeks, still much longer than the not-for-profit average run.

There is no publicly available information on revenue or profit for off-Broadway. In some cases recoupment may not be the first goal. Rodger Hess, lead producer of *My Mother's Italian, My Father's Jewish, and I'm in Therapy,* said, "A show can build up enormous equity on the road, even if the New York production doesn't recoup." Hess meant that the producer and investor share of subsidiary rights, touring productions, and regional theater stagings can eventually lead an unprofitable off-Broadway production to profit.

Commercial productions that reach break even, though, tend to publicize the fact. Take *Altar Boyz,* described in the show's publicity materials as "the hilarious account of a struggling Christian boy-band (with one nice Jewish boy) looking for their big break in the Big Apple." *The New York Times* called it "a dopey Off Broadway musical that actually works." *Altar Boyz* opened in 2005 with strong reviews, a small initial cost of one million dollars, and a weekly running cost of fifty thousand dollars. It paid back its investors but only after a three-year run. Meanwhile a production sat down in Chicago for a six-month run. Productions have played in Australia, South Korea, Hungary, Brazil, Sweden, Finland, and Japan, and the show is licensed for regional theater productions. Clearly there will be profit for the *Altar Boyz* investors.

In early 2008 the *New York Times* reported, "If there are musicals that made their money back in commercial runs Off Broadway in the last decade or so, there aren't many." In addition to *Altar Boyz,* the article mentions two that opened more than ten years before.

Estimates for the potential for financial success off-Broadway vary, but not one claims the likelihood of success is high. David Stone, producer of 2009's *Next to Normal* and 2005's *The 25th Annual Putnam County Spelling Bee,* among other shows, said, "In the last five years, there have been 120 commercial productions [off-Broadway]. Five of them have been profitable. That includes . . . *Bug* that just recouped and made a dollar-and-a-half profit. That's even scarier than Broadway."

The off-Broadway theater, both commercial and not-for-profit, offers needed variety to the New York City theater environment. However, it appears that only the rare off-Broadway production makes money in an off-Broadway venue. The chance of transfer to Broadway is small too. Fewer than one show in sixty transferred to Broadway in the two seasons we studied, 2004–5 and 2005–6.

Even Smaller Venues: Off-Off-Broadway

Off-off-Broadway refers to productions in theaters even smaller than off-Broadway theaters, namely theaters of ninety-nine or fewer seats. In early 2008 the Web site Off-Off OnLine (http://www.offoffonline.com/) listed 101 off-off-Broadway venues. Tracking off-off-Broadway venues and productions is a difficult task: they come and go.

Off-off-Broadway began as an alternative to off-Broadway once entry to off-Broadway was priced out-of-reach to many aspiring producers, playwrights, and actors. Now off-off-Broadway's identity, like that of off-Broadway, has been somewhat codified by union contracts. Off-off-Broadway shows range from professional productions which may be union or nonunion, both commercial and not-for-profit, to amateur performances. Some long-standing and highly respected off-off-Broadway companies include the Living Theatre, Soho Rep, and the Ontological-Hysteric Theater.

Off-off-Broadway productions with members of Actors Equity Association are called *Showcases*. Actors and stage managers are not required to be paid under the Showcase Code except for public transportation to rehearsals and performances. If the producer has a paying production later, there may be a contractual obligation to hire or pay Showcase actors. Total budget can't exceed twenty thousand dollars; performances can't exceed twelve in four weeks; and ticket price can't exceed fifteen dollars. All these limitations leave little cash or time for marketing. Still, in spite of the constraints, many Showcases are mounted; in 2007 Actors Equity recorded 1,045 off-off-Broadway showcases. Showcases show off new scripts that sometimes graduate to off-Broadway and actors who sometimes get hired for paying gigs.

Off-off-Broadway isn't always amateur hour. In February 2008 Kathleen Chalfont and Patricia Elliott gave eight performances of the biographical play *Vita and Virginia* at the off-off-Broadway Zipper Theatre. Chalfont has received Tony and Drama Desk nominations for *Angels in America* and the Drama Desk, OBIE, Lucille Lortel, and Outer Critics awards for *Wit*. Elliott won the Tony, Drama Desk, and Theatre World Awards for *A Little Night Music*, and she was also Tony-nominated for *The Shadow Box*.

In April 2008 a four-year-old organization, the New York Innovative Theatre Foundation, published the results of a survey of off-off-Broadway theater. The survey, certainly not comprehensive, found that 69 percent of responding organizations had existed for seven or fewer years. Most organizations produced one or two productions a year (55 percent). Eighty-five percent of productions ran for eighteen or fewer performances. About two-thirds of productions were Equity Showcases. Of those productions paying actors, 62 percent of respondents, the average payment per actor for the entire production was $420. That averages $23 per performance. Paid designers received an average of $340 per production. Only 48 percent of productions paid royalties to playwrights, averaging three percent of budget. Off-off-Broadway budgets range widely. An article in *Back Stage East*, a performers' trade magazine, cited off-off-Broadway budgets from as little as $2,416 to as much as $80,000. Rental of rehearsal space and a theater usually make up the bulk of the expense.

The foundation, by monitoring advertisements and notices, counted seventeen hundred off-off-Broadway productions in the 2006–7 season. By assuming that the survey averages are applicable to that universe—and there is no statistical reason to make that assumption, but these are the best figures available—the foundation estimated total budget for off-off-Broadway theater in the 2006–7 season at just over $31 million. Except for the rare possibility of transfer to off-Broadway or future regional production of new playscripts, there is little profit potential in off-off-Broadway.

The Royalty Pool

In the late twentieth century, royalties began to be replaced with a cumbersome construction called a "royalty pool." Reading the royalty pool stipulations in a contract can make you dizzy because of the complexity, but the idea of the royalty pool itself is easy to understand. The pool concept is that investors should receive some money any week the production is profitable, not just after recoupment of the initial investment. After fixed expenses are deducted from each week's receipts, the remainder is split between the royalty pool participants (30–45 percent) and the limited liability company. The pool is distributed based on the number of points each participant in the pool is allotted in the contracts. The pool participants are usually the same parties who might receive a straight royalty under the old system: playwright, producer, director, some designers, some star actors. The playwright is typically guaranteed a minimum payment per week but can actually make a good deal more in good weeks than he or she would have in the straight royalty system. For some as yet unknown reason, beginning in the summer of 2007 royalty pools started to disappear from commercial theater contracts in favor of traditional royalty agreements.

Many Players Make a Show

Bringing a theatrical production together always requires a lot of people with a variety of skills. The potential for big profit in a successful Broadway commercial production increases the need to be clear about responsibility and reward. Tax law, business law, and union codes must all be managed together to produce a smooth organization. Tradition has a big part to play in creating a structure that has a chance of success. Off- and off-off-Broadway need similar structures to set the baseline legal environment for a successful transfer to Broadway, the only place where there is any significant potential for profit for those involved.

Intermission

Broadway and the Shubert Foundation

Theater ownership on Broadway is an *oligopoly*. Everyone has heard of a monopoly, where one entity is the only seller of some item and, because of that, the monopoly firm can control prices and has great power in negotiations with buyers. Short of a monopoly is an oligopoly, where there are just a few sellers of some particular item. Even without outright collusion, members of an oligopoly have significant power in setting prices and buyers have little recourse. The vast majority of commercial Broadway theaters are in the hands of only three entities. The Shubert Organization owns and operates eighteen Broadway theaters, Jujamcyn Theatres owns and operates five, and the Nederlander Organization owns and operates nine.

The power of commercial theater producers to bargain with the theater owners is eroded by this oligopoly. Producers' clout is further hampered by the secretive nature of the Shubert Organization / Shubert Foundation. And the financial "Russian doll" setup of the Shubert properties—one smaller doll inside a larger doll—is made possible only by a controversial IRS ruling. It makes quite a story, but first some context.

The Shubert Organization and the Shubert Foundation

There are two related entities in charge of the Shubert theater interests: the Shubert Organization, a commercial firm that operates the businesses, and the Shubert Foundation, a not-for-profit corporation that wholly owns the Shubert Organization. This is not a situation conducive to financial transparency.

In 2005 the *New York Times* wrote, "The Shubert empire is so private—the company has no press agent or public relations department—and insular that getting a clear read on anything is next to impossible. 'It's the Kremlin in there, circa 1962,' said one dramatic artist who has worked with the Shubert Organization before (and hopes to again)."

The Shubert Organization

The Shubert Organization, Inc., operates seventeen Broadway theaters, one off-Broadway theater, and one theater each in Boston, Philadelphia, and Washington, D.C. In addition it operates what is probably the second largest internet-ticketing service in the United States, Telecharge (also called Shubert Ticketing, Inc.) Some Telecharge clients include the Jujamcyn Theatres on Broadway, Lincoln Center Theater, numerous off-Broadway theaters, regional theaters, hotels, restaurants, and more. A firm specializing in evaluating corporations that are not publicly traded has estimated that the Shubert Organization has operating revenue of $712 million yearly and a staff of two thousand.

Incidentally the largest ticketing service is Ticketmaster, headquartered in West Hollywood, with more than one-half of all ticket sales in the United States, for theaters, sporting events, and concerts. Ticketmaster is owned by IAC/Inter-ActiveCorp, a large company that also owns the Home Shopping Network and other internet and real estate companies. The size of Ticketmaster business is changing as Live Nation, the country's largest booker of popular music and other attractions, begins to sell tickets to its events through its own organization. Facing this possibility, Ticketmaster is trying to buy Live Nation.

The Shubert Foundation

The Shubert Organization is wholly owned by the not-for-profit Shubert Foundation and thus the organization does not publish its financial results. Only publicly traded corporations are required to publish annual reports. The Shubert Foundation, as a not-for-profit, makes annual IRS filings that *are* publicly available. The foundation's 2005 IRS filing (Form 990) shows total market value holdings for the foundation of $273 million. More than $100 million of that is a widely diversified portfolio of stocks and bonds.

The foundation disburses about 7 percent of its net worth each year to support "not-for-profit, professional theater and dance companies in the United States" and does a small amount of arts-related giving for education and human services. In addition the foundation maintains the Shubert Archive, "more than a century's worth of production designs, scripts, sheet music, publicity materials, photographs, correspondence, business records, and architectural plans." Unexpectedly the foundation makes unrestricted grants for general operating support. The list of recipients is a "who's who" of contemporary not-for-profit American theaters, including Lincoln Center Theatre ($275,000); the Arena Stage, Washington, D.C. ($220,000); Intiman Theatre, Seattle ($60,000); and Mabou Mines ($10,000).

The foundation's reimbursement to its officers, directors, and trustees is modest. Of the chairman, president, three vice presidents, treasurer, assistant treasurer, secretary, and assistant secretary, only the president is paid: $88,558 for five hours' work a week. All the individuals, however, also serve the Shubert Organization in high-ranking positions: board members, president, executive vice president, and vice president of finance. Any compensation from these positions is a private matter between the individuals involved and the Shubert Organization. Lawyers who specialize in not-for-profit organizations have maintained this sharing of management is a conflict of interest.

To put it another way, with the same management, the foundation and the organization are virtually the same entity. As a charitable organization, the Shubert Foundation is required to serve a public good. This service to the public is what entitles the foundation to tax-exempt status. The last Shubert family members willed the family holdings to the foundation to serve that public purpose. Meanwhile the Shubert Organization's cash flows and business dealings are hidden. Who benefits from the organization's wealth in addition to the foundation, if any do—including officers of both organizations—is unknown.

Executives for privately held corporations are accountable to the people who own the corporation. Executives for publicly traded corporations are responsible to the shareholders, who can vote them out of a job. Not-for-profit corporations are responsible to the public they serve. To ensure public accountability, not-for-profit corporations must publish their finances through Internal Revenue Service Form 990. In the curious case of the Shubert Foundation/Organization, the public has little information with which to judge how the tax-exempt organization serves the public good.

The Unknowns

In the foundation's 2005 IRS 990 filing, the Shubert Organization paid the Shubert Foundation $15 million in dividends. Why $15 million? No one knows outside the Shubert Organization and the Shubert Foundation. One might assume the amount has some relation to the profits of the Shubert Organization, but, since its books are private, there is no way to tell.

The IRS filing estimates the fair market value of the Shubert Organization at a little over $49 million, including the value of the eighteen theaters and the real estate on which they sit. It's hard to know if the fair market value stated for the Shubert Organization is realistic. Few Broadway theaters have changed hands in an arm's length transaction.

The closest comparison might be to the recent history of the Jujamcyn Theaters. Rocco Landesman bought the Jujamcyn Theaters in 2005 for $30 million. Later Landesman offered a 50 percent share in Jujamcyn for $50 million. In September 2009 half of Jujamcyn was bought by a young producer, Jordan Roth, for an undisclosed amount. His mother is the producer Daryl Roth. His father, Steven Roth, has been named by *Forbes* one of the two hundred richest Americans.

Jujamcyn owns and operates five Broadway theaters, and it has estimated yearly revenues of $24 million. By the price Landesman paid and the price he asked for, one Broadway theater is worth from $6 million to $20 million.

This recent history of the Jujamcyn sale, and offer for sale, gives a range of values to consider when looking at the value of the Shubert's Broadway holdings. By the Jujamcyn transactions, the estimated value of the Shubert's seventeen Broadway theaters is between $102 and $340 million. And that does not estimate the value of the Shubert Organization's other assets: three theaters elsewhere in the United States, an off-Broadway theater, and a ticketing service. It seems clear that the Shubert Organization is worth more than $49 million.

Of course, different pieces of real estate are never exactly equivalent. Additionally Broadway theaters are unusual pieces of real estate. Many are designated historic buildings and must remain theaters. Some have sold their air rights to developers of unrelated Manhattan buildings, earning those developers zoning approval for taller buildings than they would be eligible for without the air right.

The IRS Ruling

An unusual 1979 judgment by the IRS allows the Shubert Organization to manage great wealth while being owned by the Shubert Foundation although both structures have governing boards peopled with the same individuals. At issue was a 1979 change to tax law that forbids not-for-profit organizations from owning a controlling stake in a profit-making business. As a result more than one hundred charities divested themselves of profit-making arms. The Shubert Foundation requested a ruling from the IRS that it should not have to divest itself of the Shubert Organization because

- "the legitimate theater will be destroyed";
- new owners would likely exploit the theaters "commercially, such as for the showing of pornographic films, parking lots," or would sell them for their maximum real estate value;
- the theaters were expected in the Shubert Organization's continuing ownership to return only a "marginal profit," merely sufficient for the upkeep of the buildings.

In its request the foundation used the profits from the theaters in the decade ending in 1977, which were desperate years for the theater, to buttress the last point. The IRS concurred, ruling that the Shubert Organization was a "functionally related business" and a "program-related investment" of the Shubert Foundation. The latter designation means that the theater assets do not have to be considered when the foundation determines the minimal percentage of assets it must distribute each year to remain a 501(c)3. Again, tax lawyers believe the ruling is unsound.

In short it is impossible to estimate the value and income potential of owning a Broadway theater, for virtually all the commercial theaters are owned by non-public corporations or not-for-profit organizations. Theater owners serve as gate-keepers to the Broadway theater, deciding in many cases which plays and musicals will be seen in America's foremost theater venue. The board of the Shubert Foundation chooses who will lead the Shubert Organization, and these individuals—feared or embraced, but still unaccountable to anyone but themselves—have a major effect on the content and financial viability of commercial theater in the United States.

The Nederlander Producing Organization:
The Third Largest Theater Owner

The third major owner of Broadway theaters is the Nederlander Producing Organization with nine theaters. The Nederlander Producing Organization is privately owned and doesn't publish financial reports. In addition to Broadway theaters, Nederlander owns or operates another fifteen or so performing venues in the United States and England and produces plays, arena music events, and opera. Its estimated yearly revenue is $3.2 million.

3

●●

Risk and Return in the Commercial Theater

Since at least the 1920s, Broadway theater has been dubbed the "fabulous invalid"
—always dying but somehow never dead. Since then, theater professionals have
been concerned that the likely return from producing commercial theater was too
small to justify escalating risk. Later Robert Anderson, author of hit plays and
screenplays, put the concern with risk and return in such sharp words that they've
become a proverb: "It is next to impossible to earn a living in the theater. But you
can make a killing."

Oscar Hammerstein II was certainly a great and successful man of the theater.
Although he is popularly remembered as a lyricist and book writer of some of the
greatest musical comedies, including *Oklahoma!, South Pacific,* and *The King and I,*
he was also a theatrical producer. He came by it naturally—his grandfather Oscar
Hammerstein I was a renowned opera impresario and theater builder. Hammerstein's flop rate as a producer before he cowrote *Showboat* in 1927 was 65 percent;
before *Oklahoma!* in 1943 it was 53 percent. That is, Hammerstein never had a success rate higher than 50 percent. Yet he was considered an eminently successful
commercial Broadway producer.

More recently the producer Margo Lion said of investing in the commercial
theater, "It's like going to the track or to Las Vegas. Only 20 percent to 25 percent
of the productions on Broadway make back their initial capital." She said this despite the fact that Lion has been a producer of many wonderful Broadway shows,
such as *Caroline, or Change; Hairspray; Elaine Stritch at Liberty; The Crucible;
Angels in America; Jelly's Last Jam;* and *I Hate Hamlet.* Many of these, but not all,
earned back their initial investment and made a profit.

Despite the high likelihood of the total loss of investment, stories of profit on
Broadway abound. For example, the *New York Post* reported in the summer of 2007
that the revival of Eugene O'Neill's play *A Moon for the Misbegotten,* a limited-
run import from London starring Kevin Spacey, returned a 30 percent profit to its
investors. The investors put up $2 million to capitalize the show which closed June

10, 2007, after a run of 71 performances. A 30 percent return in less than a year—not bad. For these investors the gamble of return against risk paid off. How about more than 570 percent return over six years? That's what investors in the Broadway run of *Avenue Q* received. An initial investment of $3.5 million returned $23.5 million from the summer of 2003 to the summer of 2009.

From a financial perspective, the question remains, "Is Broadway fabulous or invalid?" Our position is that Broadway since at least the millennium is not as risky as it is popularly believed to be, although it's plenty risky. In addition there is strong information to support the premise that the potential for *profit* on Broadway is commensurate with that level of *risk*, especially when compared to some other types of investment. To establish this premise, look first at the range of revenues for Broadway runs and then the proportion of shows which recouped or lost their initial investments.

Broadway Revenues

For the seasons from 1999–2000 through 2007–8, Broadway's gross revenues were more than $7.4 billion. New productions totaled 343. At the start of this period in June 1999, twenty-seven shows were still running from the previous season. At the end of the 2007–8 season, two of the shows that were running at the start of the 1999–2000 season were still running: *The Lion King* and *Chicago*. In calculating the returns during this period, we did not include revenues received before the 1999–2000 season or after the end of the 2007–8 season. The distribution of production revenues is roughly a bell curve. In a normal bell curve, the mode, the most often occurring value, and the average value are the same or nearly so. The distribution of production revenues shown in fig. 3.1 is rather skewed. The mode is in the range of $2 to $5 million; 115 productions earned between those two amounts. Yet the average of all revenues is about $22 million. This difference between average revenue and most often occurring revenue is caused by a small number of big, long-lived hits, always musicals, that make extraordinary amounts of money.

This gap between the mode and the average revenues is relevant for the potential Broadway investor. If you were considering investing in a small show, one capitalized at, let us say, $5 million, you would be buoyed by the thought that the average Broadway production garnered $22 million in revenues. You would be concerned to learn, however, that more than one-half of all Broadway shows in this period had revenues of $5 million or less.

The Rule of the Significant Few

The top twenty earners between June 1999 and May 2008 account for more than 60 percent of Broadway's total take over a nine-season period. To put that another way, well over half of revenues during this period came from less than 7 percent of productions.

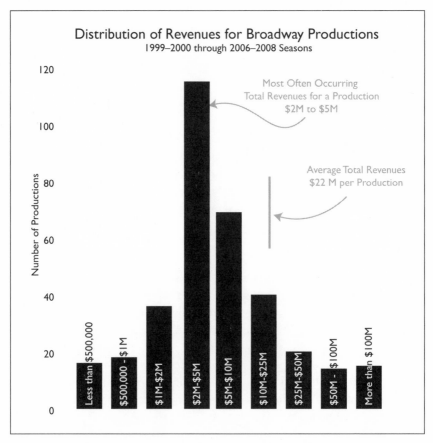

Fig. 3.1 The revenues for Broadway productions are highly skewed by the small number of very high earning productions. The difference between average total revenues and the most often occurring total revenue is telling.

This case of lop-sided revenues is an example of what business people often call the 80/20 rule. This principle is also called Pareto's law, or "the rule of the significant few." The 80/20 rule states that in many processes a small percentage of the inputs is responsible for a large percentage of the results. A retail store manager might find, for instance, that 17 percent of customers account for 85 percent of sales or that 75 percent of profit comes from 18 percent of inventory. The 80/20 rule is an admonishment to pay greatest attention not to your *average* business activities but to the *small subset of activities that result in the biggest payoffs.* Broadway illustrates the 80/20 rule when it comes to revenue: a small percentage of shows account for the lion's share of revenues (see fig. 3.2).

Some playwrights and producers have lamented the fact that the theater industry's television extravaganza, the Tony Awards, showcases big musicals at the expense of all other Broadway shows. Perhaps the organizers of the Tony Awards, the Broadway League and the American Theatre Wing, are honoring the 80/20 rule, paying the greatest attention to the small subset of Broadway that creates the greatest payoff. Or maybe it's just impossible to excerpt a great drama or comedy effectively in three and a half minutes.

Broadway Recoupment and Loss: Hits and Flops

At the end of each Broadway season, *Variety,* the entertainment trade magazine, publishes a recap, noting which new commercial productions were hits or flops. By *hit,* *Variety* means the show paid back the investors—it does not necessarily mean there was significant profit. *Flop* means the show closed without paying back all of the investors' initial outlay, although some of their initial investment may have been returned. The Broadway season runs June through May. Many shows open late in the season in hopes of winning the theater awards given in June. Because of this schedule, a large number of new productions are labeled by *Variety* as *too soon to tell.* At the end of the following season, *Variety* totes up the winners and losers from the previous season's too-soon-to-tell productions.

In the Broadway season ending May 2007, thirty-four shows opened. Eight were not-for-profit productions. Of the remaining twenty-six commercial productions, *Variety* classified four as hits, nine as flops, and thirteen as "too soon to tell"

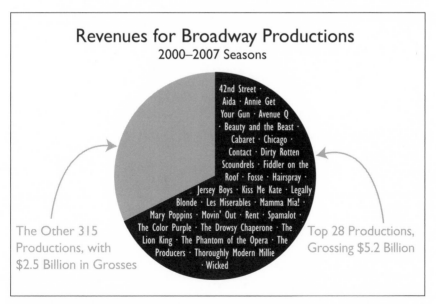

Fig. 3.2 As few as 8 percent of productions since the millennium earned two-thirds of Broadway's revenues. All of the top-earning shows are musicals. The titles are printed on the black segment of the pie chart.

by the end of the season. A year later *Variety* declared that the thirteen "too soon to tell" shows wound up as three hits, eight flops, and two still too soon to tell. The "two still too soon" were *Curtains* and *Legally Blonde. Curtains* went on to close June 29, 2008, and *Legally Blonde* closed October 19, 2008. Both failed to recoup their investments on Broadway but are expected to pay back investors from successful road tours. By *Variety*'s definition, both were flops. In sum, of 26 commercial mountings in the 2006–7 season, seven were hits and nineteen flops.

Since at least the 1960s, the often-restated rule of thumb has been that only 20 to 25 percent of Broadway productions recoup their initial investments. Producer Margo Lion, quoted earlier, repeats this approximation. In the seasons 1999–2000 through 2006–7, nearly one-third of commercial productions recouped their investments (see fig. 3.3). Note, too, that this period encompasses the time after the 9/11 attacks, when tourism and theater attendance were understandably down. The percentage of hits varied from season to season, from a low of 19 percent in 2003–4 to a high of 41 percent in 2005–6.

Loss of Investment

The table that follows shows the flops for the 2005–6 and the 2006–7 seasons—shows that did not earn back their initial investments. The flops included some major brand names and some obscure titles. Revenues accruing to flops in these two seasons ranged from $191,165 for *The Blonde in the Thunderbird*—the Suzanne Somers musical—to almost $20 million for *The Wedding Singer*. Total revenues for the 2005–6 flops were $64.8 million and for the 2006–7 flops $85.4 million. A surprising chunk of change for shows that flopped.

2005–2006 Season Flops	2006–2007 Season Flops
Barefoot in the Park	*Company*
The Blonde in the Thunderbird	*Coram Boy*
The Caine Mutiny Court Martial	*Deuce*
Chita Rivera: The Dancer's Life	*Grey Gardens*
Festen	*High Fidelity*
Hot Feet	*Inherit the Wind*
In My Life	*Jay Johnson: The Two and Only*
Latinologues	*Kiki & Herb: Alive on Broadway*
Lennon	*The Little Dog Laughed*
Lestat	*Martin Short: Fame Becomes Me*
Mark Twain Tonight!	*The Pirate Queen*
Ring of Fire	*Radio Golf*
Souvenir	*Talk Radio*
Well	*The Times They Are A-Changin'*
The Woman in White	*The Year of Magical Thinking*

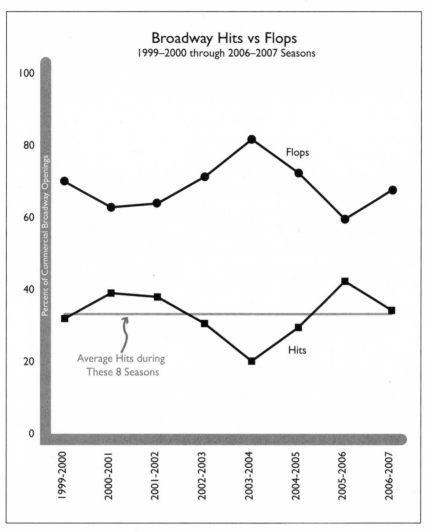

Fig. 3.3 Through the seasons, the percentage of new commercial Broadway productions that are hits and flops varies, but the average in this period was 32.29 percent.

2005–2006 Season Flops (*continued*)
The Wedding Singer
The Lieutenant of Inishmore

Because the production partnership or company lasts for multiple years and the original Broadway production shares in certain subsidiary rights, some flops do eventually return their investors' money. There's one remarkable example. In

1982 the producer David Landay raised $1.25 million to bring a stage version to Broadway of the beloved MGM film musical *Seven Brides for Seven Brothers*. The show got terrible reviews and closed after three performances. However, over the eighteen years of the Broadway partnership, the show became a staple of light-opera companies, community theaters, and student groups. By the year 2000, the original investors received the last of their money back. We must note, however, that the investors got their investment back in *nominal* dollars. Considering what inflation had done to the value of a dollar during this period, they still lost money. The $1.25 million 1982 investment was equivalent to something like $2.25 million in year 2000 dollars. Although some flops such as *Seven Brides* do eventually return their investments and even make money, such occurrences are unusual.

Opinion and Research on Broadway Success

Why do some shows run longer than others? There are many long-held opinions, but no one knows for sure. Still, statisticians and trade groups try to answer the question. The results are sometimes surprising, sometimes not.

In 2007 statisticians studied some factors to see if they correlated with the number of performances that a Broadway production enjoyed. They examined shows that opened during three seasons, 1996–97 through 1998–99, and followed the shows until the end of the next season. Because shows could still be performing at the end of their study period, they used a sophisticated measure of correlation often used in drug trials, the Cox proportional hazards model. Their findings were not always unexpected; in fact some reflected the generally understood clichés of Broadway professionals. On the anticipated side, the study found that musicals correlated with longer runs than nonmusical plays and winning a Tony Award for Best Musical or Play was linked to longer runs. No revelation here.

The big surprise was the connection of length of run to newspaper reviews. Reviews by the *New York Times* and the *Daily News* during the three-year study period were rated from positive to negative on a number scale by trained personnel, and the ratings correlated to the length a production ran. Reviews in the *Daily News* did correlate with length of run. But reviews in the *New York Times* had no significant relationship to the length of the run. This finding is stunning because the common wisdom of Broadway producers is that a *New York Times* review can make or break a show. This study shows only correlation, not causation. A positive review in the *Daily News* may not actually influence ticket buyers; it may be that the *Daily News* reviewer's judgment nearly matches the taste of the market.

continued

The 2007 statistical study had other findings, including that whether a production is a revival or an original show has no association with length of run. Common wisdom is that revivals do not run as long as original productions. There are exceptions, of course: consider the 1996 revival of the musical *Chicago,* still running at the opening of 2010. The original production of *Chicago* of 1975 ran for just over two years. In a different study, a Danish economist writing in 2004, using a different statistical method and a much larger sample, found that revivals are correlated with shorter runs.

The Broadway League—the trade group for Broadway theater owners, producers, and road producers—surveys audiences yearly. When asked what influenced the purchase of tickets, the greatest number of those responding cited the recommendation of friends, "word of mouth." Advertising motivated 38 percent. Reviews influenced 27 percent of ticket buyers surveyed. Note respondents could pick more than one influence.

Most everyone involved with professional theater believes reviews matter to the success or failure of a show, and most think that revivals are less likely to be flops but also less likely to be long-running big-money hits. Opinion and research are in agreement on the importance of a Tony Award to financial success and that most long-running productions are musicals. As economists and statisticians apply science to the question of what matters, someday definitive answers may be found.

Moneymakers: Recoupment and Profit

The ten hits of the 2005–6 season included four revivals and two new plays from London. Remember, though, how *Variety* defines a "hit": a show that recoups its initial investment. The hits of the 2005–6 season include a number of limited-run productions whose profit potential was small because of the limit.

- *The Odd Couple,* a revival of the Neil Simon comedy, starring Nathan Lane and Matthew Broderick. The comedy grossed $28.9 million for 249 performances. Limited run.
- *Primo,* a one-man show performed by the British actor Antony Sher, based on the recollections of the Auschwitz-survivor, Primo Levi. *Primo* was imported from London's National Theatre and grossed $1.9 million with 35 performances. Limited run.
- *Sweeney Todd,* a revival of the Stephen Sondheim musical, directed by John Doyle in a concept just staged in London. *Todd* grossed $22.2 million in 341 performances.

- *Jersey Boys,* a jukebox musical based on the songs of Frankie Valli and the Four Seasons, developed at La Jolla Playhouse, a not-for-profit theater in California. *Jersey Boys* is still running and doing strong business. As of January 2010, it had played 1,750 performances and grossed more than $240 million.
- *The Color Purple,* a musical based on the novel of Alice Walker, developed at the Alliance Theatre, Atlanta. *The Color Purple* ran through February 2008, playing 940 performances and grossing $104 million.
- *Bridge & Tunnel,* a one-woman show by Sarah Jones, developed through a number of not-for-profit workshops and venues. The show closed August 6, 2006, after 216 performances, grossing $5.7 million.
- *The Pajama Game,* a revival of the hit 1954 musical. This revival was produced by Roundabout Productions, a commercial venture of a not-for-profit theater. It starred Harry Connick, Jr., closed June 17, 2006, after 129 performances, grossing $8.8 million. Limited run.
- *The History Boys,* an import of a serious comedy by Alan Bennett that originated in London and touched down in New York at the end of an international tour. It closed October 1, 2006, after 185 performances on Broadway, grossing $16.7 million.
- *Faith Healer,* a revival from the Gate Theatre, Dublin, of a drama by Brian Friel, with the three roles played by Ralph Fiennes, Cherry Jones, and Ian McDiarmid. It played 117 performances and grossed $7.5 million. Limited run.
- *The Drowsy Chaperone,* a woozy musical comedy from Canada whose American premiere was at the Center Theatre Group, Los Angeles. It closed December 30, 2007, after playing 674 performances and grossing $63.5 million.

The seven hits of the 2006–7 season came from three revivals and three new productions from London. Four of the hit productions were limited runs.

- *Butley,* a revival starring Nathan Lane of Simon Grey's 1973 sour comedy. The revival was a transfer from Huntington Theatre Company. It grossed $5.4 million. Limited run.
- *A Chorus Line,* a revival of the record-breaking musical that came out of not-for-profit the Public back in 1975. The 2007 stint grossed $54.5 million.
- *Frost/Nixon,* a historical dramatization from London, had revenues of $9.4 million. A movie based on the play was released in 2008. Limited run.
- *Mary Poppins,* a stage musical developed from the Disney movie, produced by Disney and Cameron Mackintosh, imported from London. This play was still running as of January 2010, having grossed $154 million.
- *A Moon for the Misbegotten,* Eugene O'Neill's drama, starring Kevin Spacey, who brought the production to New York from London's Old Vic theater.

This work was last revived on Broadway in 2000. The 2007 run grossed $5.9 million. Limited run.

- *Spring Awakening,* a postmodern musical built on the 1891 play by Frank Wedekind. *Spring Awakening* ran until January 2009, grossing $57.4 million.
- *The Vertical Hour,* a new play by David Hare that premiered at London's Royal Court Theatre. The New York production starred Julianne Moore and grossed $7.3 million. Limited run.

Strategies That May or May Not Reduce Risk

Producers of late have tried to control the risk of new shows by adapting "name brands" established in other media, especially movies. This is a little like a strategy that marketers call "brand extension," the use of a brand outside its initial range of products or category. An ice cream manufacturer makes a deal to use a beloved candy bar as the brand for a new ice cream novelty, such as the Snickers Ice Cream Bar. Some successful versions of this strategy on Broadway are the musical theater remakes of the movies *Hairspray, Legally Blonde,* and Disney productions such as *Beauty and the Beast* and *The Lion King.* Unsuccessful versions, from the 2005–6 season alone, include *Lestat* from the Anne Rice vampire novels, *The Wedding Singer* from a hit comedy film, and *Lennon* based on the songs and life of John Lennon. Borrowing brand names from other media does not eliminate the risk of failure on Broadway.

Another approach to reducing the risk associated with a new commercial production is to stage a revival of a formerly successful play or musical, preferably with established performers, directors, and designers. Mounting a revival can be financially rewarding. Witness in the 2005–6 season *The Pajama Game* and *The Odd Couple* and in the 2006–7 season *Butley, A Chorus Line,* and *A Moon for the Misbegotten.* But revivals are not guaranteed success. Consider in the 2005–6 season the flop revivals of *Barefoot in the Park* and *Mark Twain Tonight!* and in the 2006–7 season *Journey's End, Company,* and *Inherit the Wind.* Revivals are tricky because today's social and esthetic values are inevitably different than those in place when the play was originally performed.

The budgets for revivals are different as well. Playwright Edward Albee said, "We did *Who's Afraid of Virginia Woolf?* on Broadway, in 1962, for a total cost of $45,000. Now [2005], the revival is going to cost close to $2 million. We had ticket prices at seven dollars and now they're going to be $75."

Each Broadway Show Is a New Business

Playwright Robert Anderson is correct: investors can make a killing on Broadway, but it's hard for them to make a simple living. However, we propose that the rate of failure in the commercial theater, and especially Broadway, is not unusual because each production is a *new business.* And any new business is highly prone to failure.

It's clear that a new play or musical resembles other new businesses. Story, stars, and design are all untested. Consider how the late Betty Comden and Adolph Green described the environment of a new production during an interview in 1992. Beloved lyricists whose work includes *On the Town* (1944), *Applause* (1970), and *The Will Rogers Follies* (1991) among many others, Comden and Green knew what they were talking about when they discussed working on a new Broadway show. This excerpt is from Bryer and Davison's *The Art of the American Musical: Conversations with the Creators:*

COMDEN: It's not an exact science.

GREEN: That's the phrase I was looking for! We learn, but the secret is we never learn.

COMDEN: Each time you start from a standing position. You have a new idea, a new cast, a new group of collaborators often; and every time you start anew—so there are no rules for this particular combination, this particular idea. You can learn from experience, but you can continue to make terrible mistakes.

GREEN: Yes. And no matter how experienced you are, you're still a new born babe every time you step in to that world of a show, of a work of any kind that hasn't been done before.

Roger Berlind, producer of the 2008 revivals of *Equus* and *Gypsy* and many other shows, echoed this idea but from the management end of the process: "It's like a start-up in any area of activity. You have all the problems that any other business has. . . . Every show is a new entity. It can make it or not, based on a variety of factors that you cannot anticipate." Broadway productions are as risky as all new businesses. To appreciate the risk of new business, consider a variety of kinds of new ventures. Different sources give different success rates for new businesses, but the overall story is that new businesses of every stripe are highly risky, sometimes as risky as the commercial theater.

Small Businesses

Statistics from the Small Business Administration (SBA), a United States government agency that provides support to small businesses, show that two-thirds of new employer businesses survive at least three years but only 44 percent make it to four years. Note that the SBA doesn't say whether these businesses were ever profitable. The small business owner has his or her whole wealth and ego on the line and may stick with an unprofitable business for a long time. A four-year run on Broadway would almost certainly be profitable but four years of a new small business may just be a bottomless money pit for its owner.

According to a study in the *Cornell Hotel and Restaurant Administration Quarterly*, 60 percent of new restaurants close in their first three years. And the National Federation of Independent Business (NFIB) surveys show that over the lifetime of a business, 39 percent are profitable, 30 percent break even, and 30 percent lose money.

The typical reasons given by the NFIB for new business failures include

- Insufficient capital,
- Poor management,
- Insufficient planning,
- Overexpansion.

Small business owners, like some theater investors, often have little experience in starting or operating a business. It might be more revealing to compare new commercial theater productions to the rollout of new products from established firms, companies who have been shown to understand their markets and how to develop new products. One would think, "Surely their results are better than novice entrepreneurs." That is not necessarily the case.

New Products from Established Companies

Few if any corporations report profits from individual product lines, but a search of academic journals and news magazines gives some hints about the success rate of new product introductions from successful firms.

An executive with Random House, a U.S. publishing conglomerate recently purchased by the German media giant Bertelsman, was quoted in *New York Magazine* in 2007 as saying that of eight new books Random House publishes, one makes a lot of money, one loses a lot of money and the rest hover around the break-even point. Random House is a going concern, a subsidiary of a major media conglomerate. Bertelsman's earnings before interest and taxes for 2006 were €1.9 billion (about $1.5 billion at that time); Random House earned 9.4 percent of that, or approximately $143 million.

Consider Proctor and Gamble (P&G) as reported in a 2006 edition of the *Harvard Business Review*. P&G is a global home-product powerhouse, selling brands such as Bounty, Cheer, Cover Girl, and Folgers coffee. In 2000 P&G reported $3.5 billion in earnings. But that same year P&G changed its strategy for new product development because only 35 percent of new products P&G had developed and rolled out to supermarkets all over the world met financial objectives. The new P&G strategy: reduce the money spent developing new products and instead identify growing small companies and buy the company and their developing new products. Later we will show how many commercial theater producers are taking a similar cherry-picking approach to the not-for-profit theaters.

Investor Loss vs. Charitable Contribution

There are people who will give money to commercial productions they never expect have a potential for profit. They do so because they believe the author's voice or the subject matter must be heard. They love the theater.

In terms of taxes, there is very little difference between losing money on a commercial theater production and donating the same amount to a not-for-profit theater. Individual's losses from investments can offset capital gains from profitable investments for tax purposes. If one has no gains, up to three thousand dollars can be deducted from regular income. And if that doesn't exhaust the loss, the remainder can be carried forward to be used in another tax year. The loss reduces taxes by the amount of the investor's marginal tax rate, which was as high as 35 percent in 2009. The investor still loses the money, but the IRS participates in the loss, reducing the blow. Say the loss was ten thousand dollars for an angel at the 35 percent marginal tax rate. The actual loss after taxes is sixty-five hundred dollars.

Compare that loss to what happens to the charitable supporter whose donation can offset income if deductions are itemized. The donation has a tax effect only if the supporter has itemized deductions greater than the standard deduction, currently five thousand dollars for singles and ten thousand dollars for marrieds filing together, more if over the age of sixty-five. The total of all deductions that can be made against income is limited, but any remainders can be carried forward to future years. Again the supporter has given away real money, but the IRS participates in the supporter's charity by reducing taxes. Say a supporter at the 35 percent tax rate donated ten thousand dollars to a not-for-profit theater. The actual out-of-pocket expense after taxes is sixty-five hundred dollars.

When it looked like August Wilson's play *Gem of the Ocean* would not open on Broadway for lack of investors—none of Wilson's plays, except for *Fences,* made money on Broadway—an investor ponied up $1 million, not because she thought she would receive her investment back but because she thought the play just had to be seen on Broadway. *Gem of the Ocean* ran for eighty-seven performances and grossed $2.6 million. *Variety* called it a flop.

Unlike the not-for-profit theater donor, the angel investing in an unpromising commercial production has a small but real possibility of receiving some or all of the investment back. A classic case was the celebrated Broadway production of Tony Kushner's *Angels in America* in 1993–94. The list of producers

continued

was long, and many on the list have said they backed the play because they believed it had to be seen on Broadway. The two plays recouped only about 65 percent of their $2.2 million investment on Broadway but went on to break even and earn a small profit as a result of a successful tour and other subsidiary rights.

In a 2008 interview, the CEO of P&G, A. G. Lafley, discussed the new strategy in terms of new product development: "In our industry, about 80 to 85% of new products fail. . . . Innovation is that kind of a game, and what we are trying to do is improve our success rate. And what we are also trying to do is fail earlier, fail faster, and reallocate the resources from the failures." The home-product industry, with about 80 to 85 percent of new products failing, looks little better than the commercial theater business.

A Pessimistic View from the Academic Community
and a Look at Why Good People Fail

In a discussion of venture capital, the *Harvard Business Review* is more pessimistic than P&G's CEO, offering a rule-of-thumb that 90 percent of new businesses fail, even with good plans and good people. In describing why this is, the writer proposes a statistical metaphor. Imagine that there are a number of accomplishments necessary for a business to succeed—the article proposes eight discreet steps for the sake of its discussion—and that a given business plan and group of good people have an 80 percent likelihood of fulfilling each of the number of accomplishments. A statistical naïf would say the business has an 80 percent chance of success, but that's not statistically correct. In this case the percentages are not averaged but multiplied, giving only a 17 percent likelihood of success.

To understand this result from statistics, imagine starting with one hundred people running an obstacle race with eight obstacles and each participant has an 80 percent chance of overcoming each obstacle. Failure to overcome an obstacle eliminates a person from the race. After the first obstacle, there are 80 runners left. After the second, there are 64 left. After the third, 51. . . . You get the drift. Although this discussion uses a probabilistic analogy to suggest why new businesses fail, note these are *not real statistics.*

The *Harvard Business Review* lists the individual events required for a new business to succeed to include items such as "company has sufficient capital" and "customers want product." For Broadway many essentials suggest themselves. A partial list might include

• A sizable audience is interested in the story, style, and themes of the show.
• Nothing happens in the wider world to make the show have different con-
notations. (Think how often the Sondheim musical *Assassins* was delayed
because of news events.)
• No important person in the cast gets ill or injured.
• The physical production is built for the budgeted amount, and the mechanical
scenery works.
• The creative people continue to share a vision and work in unity as the show
is developed.

Like a new business, new Broadway productions are always high risk. Even the
efforts of fabled creative people are not enough to guarantee success.

Back to Comden and Green and the Broadway theater. Despite talent, experi-
ence, and drive, they had failures, and they were asked about one of them, *A Doll's
Life.* The musical opened in 1982, and imagined what happened to Nora of Ibsen's
A Doll's House after that classic play ended. In addition to Comden and Green, the
musical had promising staff; it was directed by Harold Prince and starred George
Hearn. The musical ran for five performances.

COMDEN: I think it was just too many mistakes. There were a lot of reasons.
I don't think they thought we had any right to do anything connected with
Ibsen since we were just mere mummers from the jolly musical stage. I don't
know. It was a feminist show, and it might have hit at a little time of reverse.
GREEN: Possibly it was a little overproduced, overdone, whatever.
COMDEN: And a little gloomier than it needed to be then. . . . It ran a week
in New York. That's a really horrendous experience because it is so hard
to do a show. God knows, you don't set out to do a failure.

So, even the best creative team cannot guarantee a success. Looking at each commercial theater production as a new business is one way of understanding why
investing in the theater is risky.

None of this argument should be taken to discredit those whose talent, money,
devotion, and determination have kept the commercial theater alive in the past
and continue to do so today. This discussion proposes that *all* endeavors require
talent, money, devotion, and determination to succeed. And probably a little luck.
Show business is a difficult business, but it is still a business. A lawyer who specializes in advising Broadway producers declared, "Show business is a very personal,
highly competitive, insecure, ego-oriented business. There are other businesses
like it but none exactly like it."

Compare the outcomes of legitimate theater with those of the motion picture.
A leading economist who studies the entertainment industry estimates that out of
ten major theatrical films produced, on the average, six or seven are unprofitable

and one breaks even. As in the theater, it is the few big winners that pay for the many losers. One estimate is that 5 percent of movies account for 80 percent of industry revenues—the rule of the significant few again.

In a larger sense, we don't need to look to the financial risks and returns of specific other business endeavors to understand why so few new commercial theater productions succeed. *There is no nontrivial pursuit in which the majority of participants succeed.* The truth is that audiences for theater like audiences for all media are most interested in the exceptional, not the quotidian. You may watch Olympic runners, but not the average amateur 1,000-meter dash in your own town—unless you have a relative in the race. Audiences grow for the World Series of baseball far above the audiences for an average game during the middle of the season. The majority of new books published in any year are "okay," "average," even "mediocre." Most new television series are barely watchable. Many movies are fine to watch on a DVD in pj's with a bowl of microwaved popcorn, but not exceptional enough to get dressed and drive to a multiplex. So it is with theater. Producers, writers, directors, designers, and actors never set out to create anything less than fantastic, but inevitably the great percentage of what they create is average. For anything less than the exceptional, most audiences won't part with the cost of a Broadway ticket.

So the risk to investors in commercial theater is clearly real, even if it is proportional to the risk of investors in most new businesses. If new businesses have such a level of risk, people undertake them only because there is a possibility of substantial profit. It is hard for lovers of theater to compare a drama to a new laundry detergent or a small greeting card shop—whatever you will—but in the end, investors will go for the types of moneymaking endeavors that match the investors' needs, with acceptable returns for acceptable risks. As noted earlier, the art of the theater and its deepest meaning must be found in other books; there are plenty of them. *Stage Money* is following the money.

Financial Risk and the Promise of Profits

There is no risk-free investment. Risk is defined for investment purposes as the probability that an investment's actual return will be different than what was first expected. An investor buys common stock in a company that is earning high profits; the stock cannot be expected to earn the same profits forever. What is the probability of differing returns in the future? The probability of return different than originally anticipated is the definition of investor risk.

Typical causes of investment risk include the risk of bankruptcy, bad or corrupt management, technological obsolescence of the product, inflation, natural disaster and other acts of God, and on and on. Some risks threaten the whole value of the investment; others, if they occur, reduce the return the investment will make in the future below what was expected.

Risk is considered smaller for investments that pay a consistent return and larger for investments that pay variable earnings. Variable earnings add to risk by making an investment illiquid: an investment whose value soars and then plunges with some frequency may pay off in the long term, but if the investor needs money quickly, the value of such an investment may be low at the moment the investor must sell.

High Profit Implies High Risk

Investments inherently differ in their exposure to the elements of risk. The marketplace sets the price of an investment by considering the investment's likely return and its level of risk. The market accepts less potential profit from a low risk investment, and the market demands a high rate of return from a high risk investment. As a result investors make a higher profit by taking on higher risk. This correlation between risk and return is the vicious reality of investment return.

There are two exceptions to the rule that one can get higher returns only by taking higher risks. An investor who intelligently diversifies his portfolio can get a higher return for the average risk of his portfolio than an undiversified investor with the same level of risk. Diversity means holding investments with different levels of risk and investments whose risk comes from different sources, so all the investments in the portfolio are unlikely to be crippled at the same time. As one investment manager put it, diversification is preparing investments for many possible futures, since one cannot reliably predict the future. The second way to get a higher return is by cheating, such as through insider trading: buying or selling investments based on information not available to the general public, an action that federal law and regulation forbids.

Individual investors differ in their capacity to take on risk, depending on such things as age, total wealth, diversification, and other elements. Personality counts too: can the investor in a high-risk venture sleep at night?

Returns and Risk for Some Common Investments

To understand the effect of risk on investment return, we need to get specific about the risks and returns of some common investments. Only by looking at widely traded investments such as stocks and bonds and then at less well known things such as venture capital can the risk and returns of the commercial theater be placed in context.

Treasury notes are generally adjudged the lowest risk traditional investment. T-notes are loans made to the U.S. government. No one believes that the United States government, with its ability to tax and print money, will ever default on a treasury note. At the end of 2007, two-year notes returned 2.86 percent and thirty-year notes returned 4.39 percent to the investor.

The difference in return rate between these two notes of different duration is largely explained by the fact that, although the federal government is unlikely to default on a loan, there is still the risk of general inflation. Inflation risk is larger for a note with a longer term to maturity. Should the inflation rate rise significantly during the 30-year period of the T-note, the investor will be unhappy with the rate of return that he accepted in a low inflation period. The difference in price for notes of different duration does not make up for all possible inflation scenarios, but it is an attempt to put a price on the *risk* of these different scenarios. Should inflation stay low, the thirty-year investor will be very happy with his return. Should inflation advance a little, the thirty-year investor will be less happy but okay. If inflation skyrockets as it did in the 1980s, well, the investor took the risk. That's what risk means. The investor got a premium for undertaking the risk of the longer note—in this example, the difference between the price of the two-year note and the thirty-year note—but the risk premium does not cover all contingencies. Over a longer span, the probabilities of changes in the after-inflation value of the return increases. Long investments are thus almost always more risky than short ones.

The investor can sell the T-note at any time because there is a thriving *secondary market,* which is to say, a market for sales among investors in T-notes. However, to sell the note before maturity, the investor will have to take the price the market offers at that time, a price that will take into account the inflation rate at the time of sale and the estimate of inflation into the future. If the inflation rate rises greatly, the investor would lose capital on the sale of the note before it reaches maturity.

Municipal bonds are fairly low risk as well, although there are cases of cities defaulting on their loan payments. Highly rated municipal bonds at the end of 2007 were returning 3.08 percent for two-year bonds and 4.67 percent for 30-year bonds.

High-quality corporate bonds—loans made by an investor to a corporation— were offering an average return of 5.68 percent at the end of 2007, according to Bloomberg.com. Corporate bonds are more risky than municipal bonds or T-notes. Note that income from corporate bonds is taxed, T-note income is free of state and local taxes, and municipal bond income may or may not be taxed, depending on the activity the bond is supporting.

Common stock is considered more risky than corporate bonds, even bonds from the same company from which one might hold common stock. This is because bond payments must be made or the company goes into technical bankruptcy. Dividends to stockholders need never be paid. In the event of liquidation of a company, the bondholders are repaid from any residual value

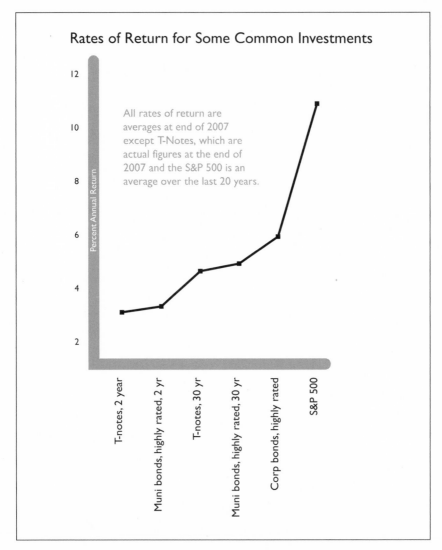

Rates of Return for Some Common Investments

All rates of return are averages at end of 2007 except T-Notes, which are actual figures at the end of 2007 and the S&P 500 is an average over the last 20 years.

Percent Annual Return

T-notes, 2 year

Muni bonds, highly rated, 2 yr

T-notes, 30 yr

Muni bonds, highly rated, 30 yr

Corp bonds, highly rated

S&P 500

Fig. 3.4 Returns increase for investments with higher levels of risk.

of the company's assets before stockholders get anything. Thus we would expect the stock market to provide a better return than the bond market. And, in the long term, it does.

The average rate of return for the twenty years between 1987 and 2007 of the Standard & Poors 500, an index of five hundred of the most widely held common stocks on the New York Stock Exchange, was 10.65 percent per year. But the rate of return ranged greatly. In the year ending calendar 2006 the return was 12.8 percent;

in calendar 2005, the return was 3.01 percent; and in 2002 the S&P 500 lost more than 23 percent. This variability in returns is a source of risk because, if the investor needs to liquidate a stock during a market downturn, that investor will take a loss.

Fig. 3.4 shows rates of return for these common investments. Economists maintain that higher returns on individual investments always entail taking on higher risk.

Markets Set Prices by Bid and Auction

How does the market come to these evaluations of the value of an investment? Not by government regulation. Rather, the actions of many investors set the rates of return. The stock and bond markets are auctions. A holder of an investment decides to sell, and a buyer wants to buy. They each decide what price is appropriate. If the buyer wants to pay too little, he'll find no sellers, and the converse is true as well: the seller who wants a price higher than a buyer is willing to pay will not be able to sell. Each may change his or her respective offer or bid until the buy and sell prices are equal and a sale can occur.

Investors will want to hold an investment that has an improved probability of future returns. Investors for such an investment are willing to pay more for it, but by paying more their rate of return is less. A hypothetical example: investor A holds a $1,000 bond that pays $100 a year in interest, or ten percent. Investor B might be willing to pay $1,100 for that bond. Investor B then receives $100 a year for the investment, but since B paid more for the bond than A, B's return is less than A's return—only about 9 percent.

For investments with a lower probability of future returns, the converse is true: market prices will fall. This is how the market as a whole, the combined actions of many independent traders, sets the appropriate price for an investment based on the market's estimate of the probable return and risk for that investment. Investors can get a higher return by choosing investments of higher risk. This relationship between risk and return means that investors getting higher returns are taking on higher risks, whether or not they have considered that fact.

The prices of the stock and bond markets are good indicators of the underlying value because these investments are traded in a generally *efficient market*. Three elements define what economists call an efficient market.

• There are many buyers and many sellers.
• The cost of transactions is modest.
• Good information is available to all interested parties at a modest cost.

The U.S. government works to make the market efficient by, among other things, requiring the promulgation of financial information from publicly traded companies and outlawing trading based on insider information. Because the public

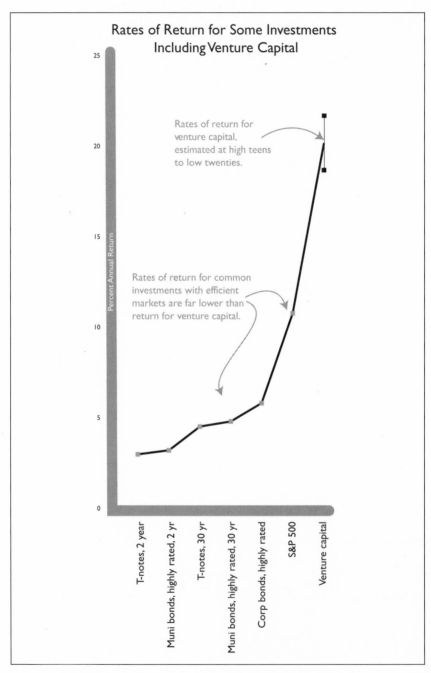

Fig. 3.5 The average rates of return for the investments reviewed so far. The risk of a variable return or of outright loss of investment determines the value of an investment.

markets for bonds and stocks are efficient, they are good evaluations of the risk and return probabilities of the underlying investments. Daily results can be and are influenced by emotion as investors respond to news of the corporations involved as well as news of the greater economy and politics, but in the long run economists consider these regulated, public markets to be sound reflections of the underlying values of the markets.

Investments without Markets

There are other investment opportunities that do not meet the standards of an efficient market, and so the association of risk and return is less precise and reliable. Investing in the commercial theater is one such venture. Before examining returns for investors in the theater, let's look at one other business plan for which the association of risk and return is less well defined: venture capital.

Venture capital (VC) firms provide capital to start-up companies that can't get funding by other means, such as bank loans or stock offerings. The start-ups can't get conventional financing because they have no income or, in some cases, no finished product yet. VC investments are very high risk, but they offer the potential for above-average returns. One of the earliest VC success stories was American Research and Development Corporation's investment in Digital Equipment Corporation (DEC, or Digital, for short). DEC was founded in 1957 by two engineers who had been working at MIT. They were developing a transistor-based computer using a huge amount of memory for that time: 64K. Digital became a successful firm. Its small computers were the most popular machines for scientific and engineering communities during the 1970s and 1980s. Digital remained a success until it was bought by Compaq in 1998, which in turn was purchased by Hewlett-Packard (HP) in 2002. As of 2006 Digital product lines were still being sold by HP.

Venture capital of about $70,000 was provided by American Research and Development Corporation to DEC when it was just a start-up. American Research and Development later sold its investment in DEC for approximately $450 million. The venture capitalists received an internal rate of return greater than 100 percent for each year of their investment.

Sounds good, you say? Where can you sign up? Not so fast! Big payouts aside, VC investing is very high risk. A recent study looked at returns for individuals who make very early phase venture investments. These people are called "angel" investors in financial writing, a sobriquet borrowed from theatrical slang for the people who invest in plays. One of the few to research these early phase investors, this study found that more than 60 percent of angel investments were totally lost. Still, 20 percent had returns of 100 percent or more. When failures are averaged in, high risk venture capitalist investment firms typically have yearly returns in the high teens or low twenties.

Successful Theater May Not Be Artful Theater

Many once successful commercial Broadway shows are not stageworthy today. Shows succeed for many reasons in addition to or other than quality. These shows ride the zeitgeist and reward their audiences in their own time and place. For example, the 1997 Broadway season had five hits according to *Variety*. The revival of *Chicago* is still running, but can you recall the others? They were *David Copperfield: Dreams and Nightmares; John Gray: Men Are from Mars, Women Are from Venus; King David;* and *Skylight.* Producer Jeffery Richards said, "You never know what will strike the imagination of the audience. . . . And it may not even be that good."

We've already established Broadway's rate of failure. Nearly two-thirds of new productions fail to pay back their initial investment. We've also maintained that investor returns must be higher for investments of higher risk. If Broadway continues to find investors, the potential for profit, when profit comes, must be very high. Is it high enough?

The Potential for Profit on Broadway

So what is an average return for investors in the commercial theater, considering both the shows that lose money and those that make a great deal of money? No one knows. Unlike the bond and stock markets, commercial theater has no entity that reports profit and loss across the spectrum of productions.

One producing group, Richard Frankel Productions Inc. (RFP), publishes its average return to an investor in its productions. With partners Marc Routh, Thomas Viertel, and Steven Baruch, Richard Frankel produces plays and musicals and provides management services to other producers. RFP's shows include big hits such as *Hairspray* and *The Producers,* modest hits such as the revivals of *Company* and *Sweeney Todd,* and flops such as *Swing!, The Triumph of Love,* and the 1999 revival of *The Sound of Music.* RFP is unusual in courting the small investor, someone with only ten thousand dollars or so to risk in a Broadway show. RFP claims that an investor who put the same amount of money in each of its productions would have lost money on some shows, made money on others, and in the end have made an annual return of 30 to 40 percent.

Broadway and off-Broadway producer Ken Davenport echoes this rate of return. His productions have grossed more than $100 million worldwide and are being produced in 25 countries. Six out of seven of his shows have returned the investors' initial investment—the *Variety* definition of a hit—and Davenport calculates that an investor who put $10,000 into each of his show would have a 40 percent return.

In sum successful theatrical producers such as RFP seem to offer returns in proportion to the risk of commercial theater investments. Fig. 3.6 shows the returns from RFP in relation to the other investments discussed in this chapter. This producing organization has an average return to investors that is even higher than venture capital's average return.

The Good, the Bad, and the Sometimes Very Profitable

There are positive things to say about *risk* and *return* on Broadway. The risk of a Broadway flop is reasonable when compared to the failure rates of new businesses and new products. We have indications that the average profit to Broadway investors seems to be commensurate with the level of risk of the commercial theater, but these are only indications. This would be a good topic for a major study to be funded by an arts-oriented philanthropy such as the Ford Foundation or the Wallace Foundation. Quantifying the risk and return of Broadway would give potential investors in commercial theater crucial data and so might attract more capital for the theater.

The negatives cannot be set aside. Unlike conventional investments, Broadway investing is done with very little information and without a real market of buyers and sellers of investments to evaluate and set the appropriate price for the investment given its level of risk. As with investments in other new businesses, the Broadway investor is placing a bet on the entrepreneur—in this case called the producer—as an individual of experience, resilience, taste, and character.

As with all high risk investments, investors should bet no more than they can afford to lose. The investor should have a diversified portfolio and substantial wealth. CitiSmithBarney refers to high risk investments such as hedge funds, investments that are illiquid and speculative, as *alternative investments,* appropriate for investors with large and well-diversified portfolios. Smith Barney doesn't include theater producing in its own list of alternative investments, but theater producing is illiquid and speculative. Various security laws require that only *accredited investors* be permitted to invest in certain high risk investments. For a ten thousand–dollar theater investment, an accredited investor has a net worth in excess of $1 million, not counting the investor's home.

It may be the case that the average novice theater investor may not be able to invest in the musicals most likely to be successes—those written, staged, and performed by proven talents. Such investments may be open only to a chosen few: friends, family, business associates. If those shows with a higher likelihood of success are taken out of the pool, then investing in the commercial theater may not be advisable for any person who can choose only from the rest of the productions.

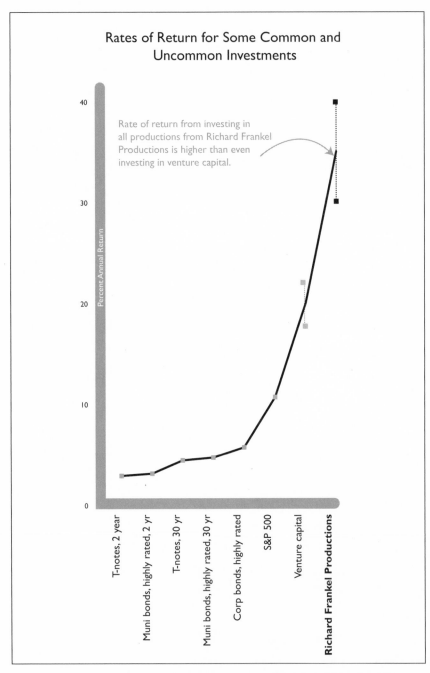

Fig. 3.6 At least one Broadway producer tracks and publicizes its average yearly return to investors, and it is higher—much higher—than other investments examined here.

Investing with Risk Is Not Gambling

Producer Margo Lion was quoted earlier comparing Broadway investing to gambling at casinos. That's not accurate. On average the casino *always* wins. The gaming business refers to *payout,* the amount of each bet on average that is returned to the gambler. For slot machines in Las Vegas, the payout ranges from 93 to 87 percent. Board game payouts are even less. If a gambler plays long enough, he will go home broke. *Broadway creates wealth* on the average. Smart investors who don't put all their money on a single bet don't have to go home broke.

Small investors in commercial theater productions get more than financial return; they also get intangible, psychic returns. Broadway has glamour. Investors get invited to cast parties and may receive tickets, CDs, framed posters, show jackets, and the like. Smart investors do not offer any money that they can't afford to lose but take heart from being involved in a medium that has an emotional meaning to them. Producer Elizabeth McCann said, "If you want to be in the theater, the fun is never knowing what's going to happen, in a million dreams, in a million years."

Intermission

The Chitlin' Circuit

There is a professional theater that flourishes away from Broadway, off-Broadway, and the not-for-profit regional theater. It's professional in that everyone involved gets paid for his work. It's entirely nonunion but has made money for many involved. No one knows how big a business it is. This theater has often been a cash-only business, sometimes funded and managed by shady individuals. Nevertheless the business has created at least one very rich crossover writer, performer, and producer: Tyler Perry.

This theater is most often called the *chitlin' circuit,* and it offers plays made by, for, and about African Americans. The playwrights are not August Wilson or Lorraine Hansberry; the best known of them include Perry, Shelley Garrett, and Michael Baisden. The play titles include *Beauty Shop, I'm Doing the Right Thing with the Wrong Man,* and *Men Cry in the Dark.* The productions are not supported by grants and donations, like those of the not-for-profit theaters that belong to the National Black Theatre Festival. The actors don't belong to Actors Equity. The scenery is sometimes ragtag. The plays are staged in large four-wall rental auditoriums of at least two thousand seats and are marketed through African American churches and radio. A production is typically dominated by one person who is producer, director, writer, and a performer.

The characters in chitlin' circuit plays can be as standardized and predictable as those of commedia dell'arte. Typical roles include an outspoken fat woman, a beautiful woman of questionable morals, an over-the-top swishy gay man, and a handsome stud. The comedy is crude, full of insults and trash talk. At some point a gospel song is belted out. At stake in the plot is the loss of a family member or friend to drugs, gangs, prison, or prostitution, and the happy ending often comes about from prayer and sometimes even from divine intervention in the form of angels or ghosts.

Why Call It the Chitlin' Circuit?

The phrase "chitlin' circuit" may have first been applied to this contemporary, nonintellectual African American theater by Henry Louis Gates, Jr., in a 1997 *New Yorker* essay. Some participants in this circuit prefer the more politically correct term *urban theater.* The use of the adjective *urban* to refer to African American culture probably began with the music business as a way to refer to R&B and hip-hop without using racial terms. It may be influenced by the National Urban League, whose mission is to enable African Americans to secure economic self-reliance, parity, power, and civil rights. The organization took the name of Urban League in the 1930s.

Historically, from the late 1800s through the 1960s, *chitlin' circuit* was the slang term for performance venues that were safe and acceptable for African American musicians, comedians, and other entertainers. Some commentators associate the term more specifically with the Theater Owners Booking Association (TOBA), a white-owned group which brought black vaudeville entertainers to black audiences in the 1920s and 30s. Theaters on the TOBA circuit included the Regal in Chicago, the Palace in Memphis, and the Lafayette in New York. At its peak in the 1920s, the circuit encompassed more than forty theaters.

The name derives from *chitlin'*, or *chitterling,* a food made of boiled pig intestines. African American playwright August Wilson—not a participant in the chitlin' circuit—described the food: "In our [African American] culinary history we had to make do with the . . . intestines of the pig rather than the loin and the ham and the bacon." Now, for some people, chitlins are a dish to be enjoyed on occasion, a reminder of one's roots in southern poverty, black and white. According to the *Oxford English Dictionary,* the origin of the curious word *chitterling* is unknown.

White people and concerns with racism are rarely referenced in these plays. Instead they deal with "matters that are of immediate concern to the . . . audience, working-class and middle-class alike: gang violence, crack addiction, teenage pregnancy, deadbeat dads. . . . They're the problems of everyday life, as real and close at hand as parking tickets and head colds," according to Henry Louis Gates, Jr., the renowned Harvard professor of African American studies.

In many cases the humor plays on some of the strongest racial and sexual stereotypes. If shown on television, these plays would be protested by civil rights groups. But the theaters in which they're performed are racially sequestered. Just as European immigrants and Yiddish speakers in New York in the early years of the twentieth century roared with pleasure at ethnic stereotype entertainment, so do the African American audiences for the chitlin' circuit plays.

The theaters where the plays are staged are usually full. The audiences, as Gates wrote "are basically blue-collar and pink-collar, and not the type to attend traditional theater." They are "styling out"—women dressed in their best church hats with matching shoes and bags and the men sporting Stetson or Dobbs hats and Kente-cloth cummerbunds or pocket scarves. Audiences are audibly stirred and may cry out "Hallelujah!" and "Testify!" The intensity of audience involvement with the stories is palpable. Gates continues, "However crude the script and the production, they're generating the kind of audience communion that most playwrights can only dream of."

James Chapmyn was a writer/performer on the circuit for a while. "I've never made so much money in my life as I made when I did the forty or so cities we did on the Chitlin' Circuit," he said. "The guy that did 'Beauty Shop' probably grossed fifteen to twenty-five million dollars. These plays make enormous money."

Beauty Shop, in fact, grossed $30 million in the 1980s and was seen by more than 20 million people according to its author Shelly Garrett. Called the "godfather of Black theater," Garrett claims one show of his took in six hundred thousand dollars a week in Atlanta. In New York, *Beauty Shop* took in eight hundred thousand a week for an eleven-week run.

Producers on the chitlin' circuit include I'm Ready Productions, AIW Entertainment, Presenting Laterras R. Whitfield, David E. Talbert Presents, Makin' It Happen Productions, Stone Ridge Entertainment, and FalkonQwest.

The crossover financial star of the chitlin' circuit is clearly Tyler Perry. Perry grew up poor and as a young adult was homeless for a while. Inspired by something heard on *The Oprah Winfrey Show* on television, Perry began writing plays. In 1998, he staged his first play, *I Know I've Been Changed,* at Atlanta's House of Blues. Cleverly he cast choir members and pastors from the area's most popular black churches in the production. He sold out eight nights at the House of Blues and two more nights at the 4,500-seat Fox Theatre. Soon Perry was doing 200 to 300 performances a year, playing to 30,000 people a week. Perry wrote, directed, produced, composed, and did makeup and set design, all to keep the budget tight. "And here we are $150 million later," he said in early 2007, "from playing that little 200-seater [the House of Blues] to arenas 12,000, 20,000 strong. It's amazing."

Perry's innovation on the chitlin' circuit formula was to play the mother character himself, all six-foot-five of him, in drag. This character, named Madea, expands the idea of the strong black mother holding the family together. Madea carries two guns in her handbag and will whip them out if necessary. She smokes grass and is blunt-spoken. "A man likes a challenge," goes a typical Madea declaration, "If you're throwing [sex] at him, sometimes he don't want to catch it."

Perry had made a small fortune—he had already built a twenty-six-room, $5 million mansion for himself in an Atlanta suburb with swimming pool, waterfall, tennis courts, and a theater—when he made Hollywood stand up and take notice. In 2005 and 2006, he made his first two films for a total budget of $11 million; each opened at number one, and together they grossed more than $110 million.

Perry has opened a movie studio in Atlanta and is building a West Coast house on twenty-two acres in Beverly Hills. His twelve stage plays have grossed more than $150 million, and DVDs of his movies and plays have sold more than 11 million copies. He even had a best-selling book in 2006, *Don't Make a Black Woman Take Off Her Earrings: Madea's Uninhibited Commentaries on Love and Life.* At the end of 2007, the cable network TBS bought one hundred episodes of Perry's comedy-drama television series *House of Payne.* Madea appears on the series now and then; more often, Perry said, if the ratings are in trouble. In 2009 Perry created a sitcom *Meet the Browns,* also for TBS.

Two films by Perry opened in 2008, *The Family That Preys* and *Meet the Browns,* which together grossed more than $77 million in their first months of release. His next film releases came in 2009, including *Madea Goes to Jail* and *I Can Do Bad All By Myself.* Altogether, his films have grossed more than $400 million. In April 2009 Perry's tenth stage play, *Tyler Perry's The Marriage Counselor,* was touring the United States and played two split-weeks—weekend performances—at New York City's twenty-eight-hundred seat nonunion Beacon Theater. Charles Isherwood reviewed the show for the *New York Times,* noting, "Mr. Perry's plays are less standard stage works than odd admixtures of gospel-pop concert, comedy show and church service. If the various elements are hardly integrated smoothly, each moment appears to satisfy on its own terms." In 2010 Perry started touring a new play, *Madea's Big Happy Family,* booking in arenas and coliseums. For example, in New York City it played WaMu at Madison Square Garden, a 5,600-seat venue with a top ticket price of $129.50. In Los Angeles it played the 3,332-seat Kodak Theatre, with a top ticket of $178.

Before Perry's crossover success, the chitlin' circuit was largely unknown to the commercial theater's family of producers, most of them white, and was under the radar of the more intellectually focused not-for-profit theater community, white or black. The true financial scope of this popular African American touring theater is unknowable, but clearly it has given some performers a good living and made some writer/producers quite wealthy.

4

The Road and Las Vegas

The touring of professional theater, colloquially referred to as *the road,* is big business. More revenue from ticket sales is collected on the road than on Broadway in a given year. Some of this money is easy to track because the trade association, the Broadway League, collects financial information from its members' tours. But the league is not the sole producer of the more than a hundred traveling shows that crisscross the United States every year. There are also educational and children's theater tours and nonunion professional tours that recycle the Broadway canon, especially musicals. All Broadway League tours must be union tours, but non-league tours are both union and nonunion.

The road, whether union or nonunion, is dominated by an entity that must be described to understand fully the structure and financial value of touring. It's now called Key Brand Entertainment: a tour producer, a tour presenter, and an owner or operator of touring venues. For completeness, consider as well Las Vegas, which has ups and downs as an important adjunct or substitute for theater touring. Together these varied strands make up the road.

The Financial Players for a Tour

As described earlier, the producer of a successful first-class production obtains an option from the copyright holder that includes a number of rights, including the right to organize one or more national tours and international productions of the play or musical. In many cases a successful Broadway run will result in the same producer organizing at least one national tour. The producer may capitalize that tour using earnings from the Broadway production or may create a new producing partnership/company to produce the tour. Unless the legal agreements with the Broadway investors stipulate how tours are to be capitalized, it's the producer's choice. Tours typically take nine months to a year to organize.

Even shows that are not successful on Broadway may spawn tours anyway. Sometimes such a tour will result in payback and profit for the original investors.

A Broadway run can create a brand name that is worthy of exploitation through a national tour even if the Broadway run itself wasn't profitable. In some cases the Broadway producer chooses to license a tour to some other producing entity. In addition producers mount revivals of musicals that have not been seen on Broadway in many years when they think road audiences are ready to see the material again.

Some producers have enough business on the road that they employ a booking agent on staff. Others engage a freelance booking agent to contract with local presenters. Booking a tour is a sophisticated task. Ideally the agent wants the best terms from each venue—the local presenter—but the agent also works for an *efficient* tour: one that moves sequentially about regions of the country—playing Atlanta, Savannah, Charlotte, Raleigh, Washington, in short order—with few long hauls between widely separated cities.

Finalizing touring schedules can take a good deal of time. The local presenters may not want to commit to a contract for specific dates for other shows before they obtain dates and contracts with the one or two blockbuster shows of the season for fear of losing out on booking those financially lucrative shows. The productions with lower expectations have to wait to finalize bookings. Successful touring relies on the kind of trust and mutual understanding that comes from continuing business relationships among the parties involved.

Additionally agents for all but the hottest productions may have to promote their offerings. The local presenter is just that, local. He or she may have a firm idea of what the market will embrace or even tolerate. Raleigh is not Chicago, and neither city is New York. Some believe the tour of *The Full Monty* struggled because middle-American audiences feared it featured male nudity. *Hairspray* includes the gimmick of the main character's mother played by a fat man in drag. *The Producers* is heavy with jokes about Jews, Nazis, and homosexuals. As one local presenter put it, "It's not complicated. Family shows play very well on the road."

Local presenters need a season of shows, a package with enough highly attractive elements to sell as a season to ticket buyers. Selling a season package financially inoculates the presenter for productions in the season that are less attractive. The best of worlds for presenters is to have a sold-out show. The best marketing is to turn a few buyers away. People want what others want. A sell-out helps sell the next show or the next season of shows. People are moved to buy in advance if they think that tickets may run out. All over the country and for all types of performances, audiences are increasingly adverse to purchasing tickets in advance, and this has decreased sales of season ticket packages. Presenters must respond to this trend through a combination of programming and marketing.

The local presenter may be an individual, a government, a college or university, a not-for-profit group that maintains a community arts center, or a consortium of regional or national presenters that book a number of venues with one contract. Presenters may own, lease, or operate under contract the space in which they present, or they may rent a space only for a series of shows.

Producer and Presenter Obligations and Contract Structure

The typical contract between a tour producer and presenter calls for the producer to provide a number of elements:

• Cast
• Stage manager and assistant stage manager
• At least some musicians
• Lead technical staff
• Company manager and press agent
• Sets, costumes, props, electrics, and sound
• Television and radio commercials, window cards, newspaper advertising, photographs, and press kits
• All rights to copyright material

The presenter agrees to provide other elements to complete the local showing:

• The theater
• Loaders for load-in and load-out of scenery, lights, and costumes
• Local stagehands and dressers
• Some local musicians
• Advertising, press, and promotion
• Front of house personnel such as ticket sellers and ushers
• Heating and air conditioning, utilities, taxes, and insurance
• Front of proscenium follow spots in most cases.

The local presenter allows the producer to sell souvenirs in the lobby, with the venue typically receiving 15 to 20 percent of the net receipts.

Touring's Three Financial Structures

The most common deal between producer and presenter is a *guarantee*. Under this structure the presenter guarantees the producer a minimum payment each week. This puts more risk on the presenter and less on the producer, but, more important for the business as a whole, it allows marginal shows to continue their tours even if they have bad weeks. Tours can collapse, leaving local presenters later in the season without a show to present. For example, in 2007 Baci Management, a theatrical booking agent with a twenty-year track record, promised productions to presenters and venues in Maryland, Virginia, and Washington, D.C. Some shows were canceled at the last minute and others with a week's notice or so. One presenter, Networks Productions in Columbia, Maryland, lost $1.2 million because of

Baci's cancellations. Even with a guarantee, the presenter's net profit is split with the producer, typically 40 percent to the presenter and 60 percent to the tour producer.

Producers sure of the box office potential of a show may want a *four-wall* deal instead. The presenter is guaranteed a set amount per week plus certain expenses for operations, but the rest of the money goes to the producer. This structure removes all risk from the presenter and—with the risk—all potential of increased profit if the local appearance is a big success. The producer essentially rents the theater—the *four-walls* of the deal's sobriquet—and takes on most expenses and profits.

A *coproduction* deal happens when a consortium or corporation of presenters fears there will be an insufficient number of appropriate shows to tour in the near future. This group then invests in new productions, in tryouts, or on Broadway to ensure that it can book the tour at a later time.

Extent of the Touring Business

The financial results of some of the players are reliably and regularly reported. For the others, one must rely on rough indicators to estimate the general financial impact of their touring.

Broadway League Touring in 2006–2007

During the calendar year 2007, twenty-one Broadway League tours were active. All but two of these were musicals. The straight plays were both offshoots of recent Broadway revivals with movie or television star performers: *Who's Afraid of Virginia Woolf?* starring Kathleen Turner and *Twelve Angry Men* headlined by Richard Thomas. The latter tour was produced by a not-for-profit theater, the Roundabout Theatre Company.

In the 2007–8 season, tours produced by members of the Broadway League grossed $956 million. In the period since the 1999–2000 season, the total grosses for Broadway and for touring presentations produced by members of the Broadway League have grown at very similar paces (see fig. 4.1). For the period from the 1999–2000 through the 2003–4 seasons, gross touring dollars trailed those of Broadway by a little. Since then Broadway League tours have grossed a few dollars more each season than Broadway.

On average, touring tickets are cheaper than Broadway tickets; in the last few seasons, the average Broadway League touring ticket price was about 74 to 80 percent of the average Broadway ticket price. In 2007–8 the league's average touring ticket price was $62.48; the average Broadway ticket was $76.37. Although the ticket price is lower, Broadway League touring productions sell more tickets each year than Broadway even though touring performs a smaller number of playing weeks. Comparing playing weeks instead of the number of productions eliminates

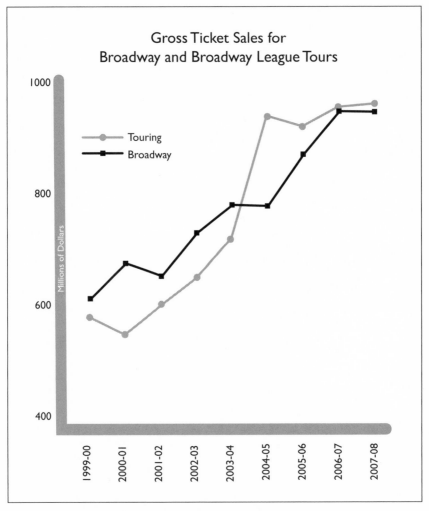

Fig. 4.1 Gross revenues for Broadway shows and for the touring shows produced by the Broadway League members are more-or-less equivalent.

concerns with length of runs or periods when a theater is *dark,* meaning unoccupied. In the 2007–8 season, for example, Broadway sold 12.3 million tickets during 1,560 playing weeks; touring shows sold 15.3 million tickets during 1,138 playing weeks. The reason for this difference: many of the theaters that house touring productions are enormous when compared to Broadway houses. The largest Broadway house is the Gershwin with 1,933 seats. Some of the large touring houses include the Chicago Theatre with 3,600 seats, the Pantages in Los Angeles with 2,703 seats, and the Fox Theatre in Atlanta with 4,678 seats.

In 2006–7, for example, Broadway League tours worked more than 650 playing weeks in eighty-nine cities ranging from Appleton, Wisconsin, to Winnipeg, Manitoba. The average stop was just more than nine weeks. But that average hides great differences. By the start of calendar year 2007, the Broadway League tour of *Chicago* was at the end of its touring life, playing only single weeks and sometimes *split weeks,* stopping in two cities in the same week. At the other extreme, the city of Chicago loved the Second National company of *Wicked* so much that the producers made the stop there open-ended; *Wicked* played Chicago for fifty-two weeks in 2007. The Third National company of *Wicked* opened in Los Angeles in late January 2007 and was still there as of the end of the year. The rest of the country had an opportunity to see *Wicked;* the First National Company stopped in other major cities such as Baltimore, Miami, Dallas, and Denver, averaging more than three-and-a-half weeks per city. *Jersey Boys* was playing San Francisco as 2007 commenced and stayed until early October. Another company of *Jersey Boys* opened in Los Angeles in May 2007 and stayed until early September. *The Color Purple* played in Chicago starting in late April and stayed until mid-October.

Tours Other Than the Broadway League

The tours produced by the Broadway League account for only a part of the touring business in America. Some nonleague tours are national; some are regional. Some are focused on college bookings or church bookings. Some are union, and many are not. Some are commercial, and some are not-for-profit. Because league members report their grosses, their touring productions are the easiest to track. The dollars earned by other tours cannot be determined, but there is interesting evidence.

All national tours of large cast, large physical production musicals that are nonleague, however, are nonunion, a conclusion based on our research. The cost of union touring is often the main reason for a tour to be produced by an entity other than a Broadway League member.

Although the Broadway League is working to enhance the value of the brand name *Broadway,* it takes no action against local presenters who use the term even for tours that have no recent connection with Broadway. Communities across the United States have local seasons called "Broadway in Cincinnati"—fill in your city name—which present some League tours and some non-League in the same "Broadway in . . ." season.

In a few cases a producer may decide that a show that failed on Broadway has appeal for the touring market outside of Manhattan. One instance is the Ahrens and Flaherty musical *Seussical,* which flopped on Broadway in 2001. It lost $10.5 million. For the tour the show's physical production was scaled down, and the songs and script were altered to be closer to the qualities of the original material, the children's books of Dr. Seuss. "We thought there was a really good show there, and for whatever reason it wasn't recognized on Broadway," said Ken Gentry, the president of the producers, NETworks Presentations. "While that may or may not appeal to a New York audience, I was fairly certain that would appeal to an audience across the country." This altered *Seussical* was a critical and financial success on the road, playing in Philadelphia, Houston, Milwaukee, Cincinnati, and elsewhere. In Cincinnati, for example, the show grossed more than five hundred thousand dollars, earning the local presenter a profit. The musical *Little Women* also saw success on the road, recouping the $7 million it had lost on Broadway. There's no guarantee that a musical that failed on Broadway will have appeal to the touring audience. For instance *Saturday Night Fever* did little better financially and critically on the road than it had on Broadway.

Disney is not a member of the league, but it regularly tours shows with no intention of bringing them to Broadway. When the cable movie *High School Musical* became a phenomenon, for example, Disney put a touring production on the road as soon as possible. Also an ice show, a rock-concert styled tour, a television sequel, and a second sequel released as a theatrical movie. As noted in "Intermission: Disney on Broadway," the company's great strength is to market brand names across many media and in physical forms such as toys, clothing, and games.

To help understand the scope of the nonleague touring business, we attempted to identify most of the nonleague tours on the road during calendar year 2007. To do so, we searched through sixteen months of casting notices published in *Back Stage East,* which calls itself the "actor's primary resource." *Back Stage* publishes between eight hundred and one thousand casting notices each week for every type of performance. *Back Stage East* is published by Nielsen Business Media, a branch of the Nielsen Company, an international firm best known as one of the two businesses that track television ratings. The Nielsen Company is a privately held firm with revenues in excess of $4.7 billion. This search for tour information may not be exhaustive, but it indicates the general size of the nonleague touring market. In the period from June 2006 through October 2007, there were auditions for seventy-eight tours published in *Back Stage,* not including auditions for Broadway League-produced tours.

Children's Theatre and Educational Tours

At least twenty-two tours were shows aimed at children in 2006–07, ranging from national tours of established brands such as *Dora the Explorer Live!* to regional tours like *Happy Holidays around the World.* An additional eighteen tours were educational tours, aimed at public schools and colleges. These included a five-state tour called *Shakespeare Live* prepared for middle and high schools and *Sex Signals,* a show developed for college students intended to enhance their understanding of their own sexual responsibilities.

Some of these touring children's shows are big business. The *Dora the Explorer Live!* shows, produced by Nickelodeon and the presenter Broadway Across America, have grossed more than $85 million in sales worldwide, traveled to more than 255 markets across North America, Europe, Asia, Australia, and Southeast Asia, and been seen by 2.7 million.

Touring by Not-for-Profit Theaters

A small number of additional tours were not for profit; many of these largely seek bookings from educational institutions. These organizations include the Acting Company, the American Conservatory Theatre, the Montana Repertory Theatre, and the American Shakespeare Center.

The Acting Company says it "promotes theater and literacy by bringing a touring repertory of classical productions, talented young actors and teaching artists into communities across America, particularly those where live performance and theater arts education is limited or non-existent . . . performing each year in over 50 cities to audiences of 70,000 and reaching more than 25,000 students with its arts education programs."

The American Conservatory Theatre, located in San Francisco, produces and runs a conservatory for actor training. Out of that, it produces a tour for its geographic area. Connected with the University of Montana, the Montana Repertory Theatre was established as a professional touring company in 1967, providing professional theater to Montana and neighboring states. Located in Staunton, Virginia, the American Shakespeare Center presents Shakespeare's plays there in a re-creation of the first English indoor theater, the Blackfriars Theatre. They tour part of the year on the East Coast, playing mostly in university venues.

Large, National, Nonleague, Nonunion Musical Tours

What remains from the survey of nonleague tours are national tours of musicals whose producers, at least, consider them to be comparable in quality to those produced by the Broadway League. In 2007 there were at least eighteen such tours, all nonunion. There are three dominant entities in large nonleague, nonunion touring—NETworks, Big League Theatricals, and Troika Entertainment—and a number of "bit players" who produce one or two tours a year.

Among the small number of producers to mount one show a year is Candlewood International. It toured *Camelot* in October and November 2006 and from February to April 2007, with most performances as one-night stands. Columbia Artists Theatrical, a division of Columbia Arts Management, Inc., toured *Dirty Rotten Scoundrels*. This nonunion tour began within three weeks of the close in August 2007 of the First National Equity tour of *Dirty Rotten Scoundrels*, which had been produced by a member of the Broadway League. The nonunion tour closed by March 2008. Music Theatre International toured *Wonderful Town,* and Windwood Productions toured *Urban Cowboy.*

Prather Entertainment Group, a company that runs three dinner theaters, also tours one production a year, and in 2007 it was *Beehive,* described as "a high-energy musical revue tracing the coming of age of women's music through 37 popular hits of the girl groups and solo singers of the 1960's" such as the Chiffons, the Supremes, Tina Turner, and Aretha Franklin. Prather tours typically play one-, two- , and three-day engagements in towns such as Marion, Ohio; Platteville, Wisconsin; Greenwood, Connecticut; Waco, Texas; and Joplin, Missouri.

The nonleague, nonunion tour of the musical *Avenue Q* was produced by a partnership called Q Tour Limited. *Avenue Q* started touring June 30, 2007, in San Diego. The second national tour played fifty cities in the first half of 2010. Two tours were produced by Phoenix Entertainment, a revival of *Gypsy* and a tour of the Broadway-flop musical based on Johnny Cash's music, *Ring of Fire.* Phoenix has produced about seventy-five tours in nearly thirty years in the United States and Asia. Phoenix tours typically play one- to three-night stands.

The dominant producers for nonunion tours are NETworks, Big League Theatricals, and Troika Entertainment. In 2007 Big League was ending a nonunion U.S. tour of Disney's *Aida,* as well as pursuing international tours. *Aida* has never had a union national tour. Big League, located in Maryland, has produced theatrical tours for more than twenty years. Big League is a subsidiary of Dodgers Theatricals, a major Broadway League producer, which has been behind Broadway shows such as *Jersey Boys, Urinetown,* and *The Farnsworth Invention* and Broadway revivals of *Guys and Dolls* and *Into the Woods.*

NETworks Presentations, LLC, was founded in 1995 and has produced and managed more than two dozen shows. As a limited liability corporation, NETworks Presentations is not required to file annual reports or a tax return. Thus little information is available about NETworks' size or revenues. In 2007 NETworks was touring *Annie, The Wedding Singer, The Producers,* and *Hairspray.*

Troika, a privately-held corporation, is headquartered in Washington, D.C., and promotes itself as "thinking outside the apple," meaning outside of New York City and Broadway. In addition to United States tours, Troika produces tours for Europe and Asia and shows for casinos. They've been in business more than twenty years. *Reference USA,* a general business information source, estimates annual sales at $2.5 to $5 million. Troika tours typically stand for one, two or three nights. Troika was moving *Evita, Jesus Christ Superstar, Movin' Out,* and *Cats* about the country in 2007.

These nonleague, large-scale musicals fall into three groups:

- Revivals not connected to recent Broadway outings;
- Second or third tours of relatively recent Broadway shows intended to play markets smaller than the Broadway League tours did, often with one-night stands or split-weeks;
- Tours of shows that were not hits on Broadway.

Some of the revival tours are picked up by U.S. producers from regional British tours.

Variety noted that what it was calling *road-only productions* "are also emerging as crucial potential profit centers for presenters squeezed by the terms demanded by the blockbuster titles." These shows are cheaper and often more family-focused than are the Broadway League first national-tour shows. They are booked under guarantees of less than three hundred thousand dollars per week, providing economic incentive for local presenters to schedule them.

In sum non-Broadway League touring spans an enormous gamut, from short-lived educational shows aimed at public schools, to coliseum kid-pleasers that grew out of Public Television programming for children, to nonunion tours of recent or revived Broadway musicals. Comparing just the non-Equity musicals to the league's, in number and estimated total playing weeks, leads to the conclusion that in calendar year 2007 non-Equity tours grossed somewhat less than one-half of what Broadway League–produced tours did. Still that is an attractive size market of about $300 million or so.

Nonunion Tours: The Controversy

As the nonunion touring business grew, eventually Equity could no longer overlook the competition these tours presented to its membership. Equity focused on nonunion tours beginning in fall 2001, when the first tour of the Broadway revival of *The Music Man* was organized by Big League Theatricals as a nonunion tour. Dan Sher, a Big League executive, said the revival was "simply too big and expensive to tour," so Big League was granted the license to tour the show using cheaper, non-Equity actors.

Equity hadn't been thrilled about nonunion tours before this time. But *The Music Man* tour upped the ante at stake: it was to be a *first national tour,* playing twenty cities, including Seattle, Atlanta, and Chicago, in fewer than ten months. Equity noted that the size of *The Music Man* cast—thirty-two plus a standby and six all-purpose chorus understudies, called *swings*—was not large compared with shows that successfully toured with Equity contracts, such as *Les Misérables* and *The Scarlet Pimpernel.* Tickets for the nonunion tour, Equity pointed out, were priced as high as union shows had been. In most cities the nonunion tour would

> ### First National Tour and Bus-and-Truck Tour
>
> At one time, a distinction was made between the first national tour and sub-sequent tours, sometimes called *bus-and-truck* tours.
>
> Bus-and-truck tours were less expensive, with less scenery and costumes and less well-known performers. They played shorter stops, in smaller cities that couldn't support a long stay by the First National tours. They moved about the country, performers in buses and the scenery in trucks, hence the name. First National tours moved by train—far swankier at the time.
>
> Tours are still styled by their producers as "First National," "Second National," and so on, but the terms have little of the cost and quality distinctions they once had. Almost all scenery moves by truck—the first national tour of *The Phantom of the Opera* used more than 20 trucks—and performers, unless they negotiate airfare in their contracts, move by bus.
>
> A more contemporary distinction might be between tours produced by members of the Broadway League and other tours. But in the United States, outside New York City, the word *Broadway* is used very loosely. Another important distinction today is between Equity tours and nonunion tours. Both distinctions are discussed in this chapter.

be billed as being a Broadway show, and Equity argued that a Broadway show was a union show.

Equity mounted a boycott of the tour after the tour's producers refused to negotiate a special contract that would have allowed Equity actors to appear in *The Music Man* for less than the union touring rate. Equity handbills were distributed in Orlando, Chicago, and Seattle. The boycott was supported by the AFL-CIO, the American Federation of Musicians, the American Federation of Teachers, Screen Actors Guild, the American Federation of Television and Radio Artists, and other labor groups. The boycotts had little effect on attendance, however.

In 2002 Equity organized against a Big League Theatricals tour of *Miss Saigon*. This Big League Theatricals tour was not the first tour of the property; an Equity tour had played eight years. The next year, in a lead-up to the contract negotiations with the Broadway League, Equity began rallying its members against nonunion tours. Alan Eisenberg, Equity's executive director, noted that 60 percent of all touring shows were Equity in 2003, down from 90 percent just ten years before.

In the 2004 contract, Equity and the Broadway League agreed to a new experimental touring program. The experimental tours would be entitled to a lower wage than standard Equity tours, but in return the actors would share in any profits the tour made and their wages would increase once a tour recouped its initial investment. To police the new agreement, producers under the experimental program would have to supply Equity with detailed financial information on the experimental productions. The new contract appears to be working in the union's favor. Equity's figures in its 2007 annual report show that total union work weeks for tours, which had been declining before the new contract, increased by 32 percent from the 2002–3 season to 2006–7. Meanwhile almost seven thousand work-weeks were covered under the experimental tour contracts in 2006–7.

Under a standard production touring contract for 2009–10, Equity actors receive a minimum salary of $1,605 per week; producers pay a per diem to the actors for housing and meals of $833 per week and pay $165 per actor per week to Equity's health insurance. Under the experimental touring contract, minimum salaries range from $745 to $1,303 per week plus per diem of $728 per week, and the producers pay $89.50 for health insurance.

Salaries for nonunion tours are hard to discover; most producers of these tours are reticent to comment on the issue. However, Seth Wenig, executive producer for NETworks, did offer some figures for NETworks' nonunion tours: "Salaries vary depending on the role. . . . On average, we pay anywhere between $850 and $1,750 per week" and per diem is up to $500. NETworks offers a flex health plan, $50 a week to apply to the actors' own insurance.

Nonunion touring actors are usually younger than Equity actors, and some believe the nonunion staff are being exploited by the nonunion tour producers. For instance Equity actors are not required to perform on days with significant travel time; this exemption is not the case for nonunion actors. And, in some limited cases, nonunion actors may be expected to pitch in for load-in and load-out of scenery, lights, and costumes. In 2003 then–first vice president of Actors Equity, Mark Zimmerman, told a rally in New York City's Duffy Square, "Across the country, theaters are misleading their subscribers by describing their seasons as 'Broadway series' when those shows include non-Equity tours. It is time for those theaters to stop cheapening the Broadway brand by using it to describe shows that do not compensate the actors, stage managers, and all other show personnel as professionals. It is time for producers to stop the economic bullying of young actors who are trying to build their experience and resumes."

With its contract negotiations and boycott clout, Actors Equity Association has done a lot to unionize the touring market. Still research demonstrates that, as late as the 2007–8 season, there were many U.S. communities, large and small, giving financial support to nonunion tours.

The Only Large, Vertically Integrated Touring Company Changes Hands

For many years a substantial portion of nationwide touring was dominated by one company—as sometimes a presenter, a producer, a venue owner, or all three—although that company regularly changed ownership and names along the way.

The company in question started twenty-five years ago as a division of Pace Entertainment, was then sold to an aggressive company called SFX Entertainment, which in turn was bought by the enormous entertainment and marketing conglomerate Clear Channel, which spun off part of itself, including theater touring, to make Live Nation. In 2007 Live Nation sold a part of its theater-touring holdings to the Nederlander Organization and Madison Square Garden Entertainment, the live entertainment division of Cablevision Systems Corporations. In 2008 Live Nation sold the rest of its theater tour business to Key Brand Entertainment. At the time of this growth and economic activity, the ascendancy of big, entrepreneurial business into the world of traditional touring was seen by some as the salvation and by others as the beginning of the end for theatrical touring. In fact the big money, big corporation folks found that touring is enslaved to two things: the economy and the development of enticing theater musicals that are marketable to middle-American audiences. Booking shows is a local business, and successful presenters know their own markets in an intuitive depth that a national firm can never match. Along the way of these acquisitions and de-acquisitions, a lot of money changed hands. The amounts of money help identify the value of theatrical touring in the United States.

PACE Theatrical

PACE started in Houston as a promoter of an annual boat show. It grew into producing rock concert tours, managing outdoor amphitheaters, and producing monster truck shows. In 1981 it started the PACE Theatrical Group, which by 1990 was originating the majority of theatrical productions on the road. By 1998 PACE Theatrical managed subscription series in twenty-six cities and had offices in Houston, New York, Los Angeles, and London.

In 1998 PACE was bought by SFX, at a cost of $130 million. At the time it was acquired, PACE was estimated to be the largest privately owned entertainment company in the world. This acquisition made the traditional, independent theater tour presenters nervous. "If SFX puts all the different pieces together," said one rival of PACE speaking on condition of anonymity, "they are bordering on a monopoly of the Broadway road."

Thespians with knowledge of history would have been concerned because they knew about former tour monopolies. The Theatrical Trust, also called the Theatrical Syndicate, under Abe Erlanger and Mark Klaw was a theater management firm of the 1890s that exercised monopolistic control of touring theater and entertainment. The syndicate's high-handed treatment of performers was a major reason for the establishment of Actors Equity Association in 1913. The Shuberts overtook the Theatrical Trust in about 1916 and were the monopolistic force in theater touring until 1956, when an antitrust suit forced them to divest themselves of a

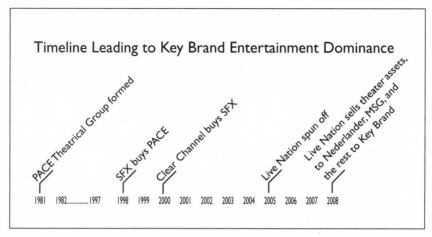

Fig. 4.2   Since 1998 the dominant corporation in theater touring has changed multiple times.

number of theater holdings. The history of the first sixty years or so of theatrical touring in the United States, then, was a story of repeated monopolization, with little or no room for the independent or emerging presenter.

Tony Micocci, in his how-to *Booking Performance Tours,* notes, "The conglomerates are the *elephants in the room,* and a thumbs down from [the large touring conglomerate] on a production can well mean that an insufficient volume of touring is available . . . to make a tour financially viable. . . . A thumbs up is no guarantee that the producer will receive the terms sought as [the conglomerate] is in a strong position to establish price."

SFX Entertainment Buys PACE

The founder of SFX Entertainment, Robert F. X. Sillerman, made his first success in radio. If that striking name seems familiar, much later Sillerman joined with Mel Brooks to produce *Mel Brook's Young Frankenstein: The Musical,* which closed on Broadway in January 2009 without recouping its investment. From radio it seemed a natural step to invest in concerts, which SFX did in the late 1990s, and then it spread to Europe and began building sports franchises. It saw its conglomeration of businesses as a marketing powerhouse: advertising on radio, at sporting events, and through sponsorships of rock tours. Along the way SFX acquired PACE Entertainment and parts of smaller entities in theater touring. Although SFX and its successor, Clear Channel, affected the touring business by their sheer size, they were not primarily interested in theater touring; they sought a conglomeration that maximized what was essentially an advertising business.

Clear Channel Buys SFX Entertainment

In 2000 Clear Channel bought SFX for $3.3 billion in stock and the assumption of $1.1 billion in debt. Prior to the purchase, Clear Channel owned or programmed for more than 435 radio stations in about 100 U.S. markets; it was the second-largest radio-station owner in the country. Also it was one of the world's largest outdoor advertising companies, with more than three hundred thousand outdoor advertising displays in the United States and fourteen international markets.

But Clear Channel's dominant position in theatrical touring did not make consistent profits in its first five years. Independent producer Tom Viertel noted at the time, "The theater business belongs in private hands because it can't grow with any consistency. The nature of the product flow is so unpredictable." Publicly held companies such as Clear Channel pay a high price in lowered stock values as a result of inconsistent earnings. As noted earlier, inconsistent earnings are considered higher risk by stock market investors, so they bid down the price of a company with variable earnings.

Live Nation is Spun-off from Clear Channel

Live Nation, a publicly held company specializing in live presentations including concerts and theater touring, was spun off by Clear Channel in 2005. In that year Live Nation promoted or produced more than 28,500 events, including music concerts, theatrical shows, specialized motor sports, and other events, with total attendance exceeding 61 million. It owned or operated 117 venues, consisting of 75 U.S. and 42 international venues, including 39 amphitheaters, 58 theaters, 14 clubs, 4 arenas, and 2 festival sites.

At the time of the spin-off, Live Nation stock was valued at $11 a share. With more than 67 million shares outstanding, the market valuation of Live Nation was better than $735 million. For calendar year 2005, Live Nation's global theater business generated approximately $317 million, or 11 percent, of its total revenues. The theater business might have an estimated market value of about $80 million, derived by multiplying Live Nation's market capitalization by the percentage of revenue coming from theater touring. A much smaller theater touring competitor estimated that year that Live Nation represented about one-third of Broadway touring attendance.

From the start Live Nation CEO Michael Rapino stated that theater was not a personal interest of his. By the end of 2008, Live Nation was essentially out of the theater-touring business. In late 2007 Live Nation sold 50 percent of its interest in a Chicago tour presenter called Broadway in Chicago to the Nederlander Organization for $60 million; Nederlander already owned the other half. The deal included ownership of Chicago's Oriental Theater.

Off-Broadway Touring

In 2005 Orin Wolf founded Off Broadway Booking, a touring organization focused on smaller, sometimes edgier shows, many of which played off-Broadway in New York City. The first season included *History of the World,* a hip-hop influenced staging about the power of speech, and a revival of the musical *The Me Nobody Knows,* a show that ran for more than two hundred performances off-Broadway in 1970. It was inspired by the anthologized writings of nearly two hundred New York City students aged 7 through 18 and was subtitled "Children's Voices from the Ghetto."

In addition Off Broadway Booking planned a smaller tour of college venues for the off-Broadway two-hander *Matt & Ben,* a "deliciously spiteful send-up of Hollywood's naked emperors" according to *The New York Times* review. *Two-hander* is the term for a show with two actors. Since its first year, Off Broadway Booking has toured shows including *Gilligan's Island: the Musical; My Mother's Italian, My Father's Jewish, I'm in Therapy;* and *The Great American Trailer Park Musical.* The revenues for these tours are not reported.

Key Brand Entertainment Buys Most of Live Nation's Theater Touring Holdings

The rest of Live Nation's theatrical division was sold to Key Brand Entertainment (KBE) in 2008 for $90.4 million. KBE acquired the presenting organization Broadway Across America, eight theaters in the United States and Canada, and investments in thirteen current Broadway shows and eight touring productions. Key Brand Entertainment, Inc. is a private investment company dedicated exclusively to the development, production, and distribution of live theater, owned and controlled by British theater producer John Gore.

KBE now describes Broadway Across America as a presenter of "first-class touring Broadway musicals and plays, family productions, and other live events throughout a network of 43 North American cities. Broadway Across America is also dedicated to the development and production of new and diverse live theater for productions on Broadway, across America, and throughout the world." John Gore's biography notes that he "has been involved in both the West End and Broadway for almost twenty years. He became the largest shareholder in the original *Cats* and *The Phantom of the Opera,* as well as investing in all the other shows of Andrew Lloyd Webber." On Broadway, Gore and KBE have coproduced several recent shows, including the 2007 revivals of the French farce *Boeing-Boeing* and

Equus starring *Harry Potter* film star Daniel Radcliff, as well as the 2009 revival of *West Side Story.* It's too early to determine what effect a large corporation, focused solely on live theater, will have on Broadway and the touring business.

Las Vegas

The Broadway theater area—actually several blocks near the intersection of Broadway and 7th Avenue—has been called the "Great White Way" in tribute to all its glittering lights and neon. The revitalized Broadway area of today is brighter than it ever was. It's a sight! But when it comes to neon and glitz, Broadway has nothing on the Strip in Las Vegas.

The Strip, about four miles on Las Vegas Boulevard South just outside of the city limits, boasts many of the largest hotels and casinos in the world. These enormous properties emit an otherworldly glow at night, beckoning tourists and their gambling dollars. New casinos now have to have a gimmick, and so you can ride a gondola at the Venetian, visit Paris, where a somewhat reduced copy of the Eiffel Tower pokes out of a copy of the Paris Opera House, sleep in the black glass pyramid that is the Egyptian-themed Luxor, or nosh on hot dogs or corned beef in the Disneyland-like streets of the New York, New York Hotel and Casino.

In addition to eye-catching décor, well-priced buffets, and expensive outposts of world-class restaurants, every big casino of late has required a standing-room-only performance extravaganza. Sometimes their theaters have been filled with brand names from Broadway. And sometimes Broadway shows have failed to provide the casinos with the draw the casinos' management required, leading to the shows' closure.

Not everything that appears in a theater *is* theater, at least according to Actors Equity Association, and most observers would agree. Las Vegas has singers and dancers, topless burlesque, and magicians: this is not theater but what the entertainment business would call *variety arts.* The American Guild of Variety Artists is a union representing performers in the circus, Las Vegas showrooms and cabarets, comedy showcases and magic shows, dance revues, and theme parks. That list of venues can serve to define variety arts. The term also applies to what Cirque du Soleil does so well around the world and especially in Las Vegas. Cirque du Soleil's trademark, an eye-popping combination of fantastic stage design and lighting spectacle, dance, and music with the traditional circus acts of Europe and Asia, had six shows running in Las Vegas in 2010: *Mystere, O, Zumanity, Ka, CRISS ANGEL Believe,* and *Love.* Worldwide more than 10 million people saw a Cirque du Soleil show in 2008.

Cirque du Soleil shows are not theater, and Equity has made no attempt to unionize their performers. A spokesperson for Equity explained why: "Their show doesn't have a book (script) and consequently wouldn't fall under our jurisdiction." Compared to the great financial success of the Cirque productions,

Broadway shows in Las Vegas have never been more than a small presence. The most recent recurrence of the fad for Broadway shows in Las Vegas casinos was sparked by the success of *Mamma Mia!,* which had a six-year profitable run, 2002–8, at the Mandalay Bay Hotel and Casino. *Mamma Mia!,* the jukebox-musical built around the worldwide 1970s hits of the Swedish pop group ABBA, opened first in London. The musical has played Berlin, Barcelona, Oslo, Moscow, Athens, the Netherlands, and who knows where else. The Broadway incarnation was running as 2010 dawned; it opened in 2001. Starring Pierce Brosnan and Meryl Streep, the movie based on the musical was an enormous success in 2008, grossing more than $500 million internationally.

But if the success of *Mamma Mia!* led casino owners to believe that any Broadway hit would work in Las Vegas, they were deceived. For *Avenue Q,* the adult puppet show, casino owner Steve Wynn paid $5 million for an exclusive license to produce it at his Wynn Las Vegas hotel. The production was a failure, closing after a run of nine months. Although profitable while it ran, *Avenue Q* didn't fill the $40 million, twelve-hundred-seat house Wynn built for it; it ran usually at 50 percent of capacity. Wynn's house has about 40 percent more seats than the show had to sell at its Broadway house. When *Q* didn't immediately sell out, the writers shortened the work, under Wynn's request, to run at 90 minutes with no intermission. The show was aggressively promoted, even to the extent of dressing twenty cabs in orange fuzz like the fur of the onstage puppets. It didn't help draw fuller houses.

Casinos expect shows to draw people into their hotel rooms and their gaming tables and slots, so only packed houses will do. For example, producers of another Las Vegas show have determined that about one-third of their theater audience stays in the show's hotel. Wynn had a follow-up: he had paid a reported $10 million to have the exclusive license in three states—California, Arizona, and Nevada—for the Monty Python musical *Spamalot.* But *Spamalot* at Wynn's casino had its last night July 13, 2008, after a fifteen-month run.

Meanwhile the Las Vegas version of the Broadway hit *Hairspray* lasted only four months, closing in 2006. In May 2009 *Variety* reported that a ninety-minute version of *Hairspray* was licensed to play on Royal Caribbean's new cruise ship *Oasis of the Seas.* The ship has a capacity of 5,400 guests and a theater seating 1,350. An import of the boffo London show *We Will Rock You,* a jukebox musical based on the music of the rock group Queen, lasted just eleven months. Incidentally *We Will Rock You* has not played Broadway despite running more than six years in London's West End. A version of the Andrew Lloyd Webber international hit *The Phantom of the Opera* played at the Venetian as 2010 began. Shortened to about ninety intermissionless minutes and renamed *Phantom: The Las Vegas Spectacular,* the show is rumored to be drawing poorly. Insiders expect it to shutter soon. It opened in June 2006. "I persist in thinking that Las Vegas is pretty much a cyclical thing," said Broadway producer Tom Viertel. "We've been through two or three periods in my lifetime when Broadway shows were a big thing in Las Vegas. Then a couple of them fail, and the whole thing disappears for a while."

Why is Broadway only rarely *boffo* on the Strip? Tony Awards and reviews mean little in Las Vegas, where the potential audience turns over virtually 100 percent every three days. Those attracted to Las Vegas include many folks who are not theatergoers in their hometowns. The audience and artistic conventions of the theater are different from those of television or rock concerts. Many visitors to Las Vegas are foreigners, and shows that rely on language may not be attractive to them. This last bodes well for the run of the jukebox musical based on the music of Frankie Valli and the Four Seasons, *Jersey Boys*, which opened in Las Vegas at the end of 2008, and was still running in March 2010. Finally, in a market that doesn't follow Broadway awards or reviews and turns over regularly, brand names are all important.

Success on the Road and Las Vegas Requires Local Knowledge

Las Vegas is not unlike the traditional theater touring market. Both the road and Las Vegas are *local* businesses where local presenters rely on their knowledge, even if just intuitive, of their own markets. A broad brush to marketing, a national approach, often fails. As said by the traveling salesmen in the opening number of the great American musical *The Music Man*, "You gotta know the territory."

Intermission

Playbill

If you attend a professional theater production in the United States, there's a good chance the program you receive will be *Playbill.* This small glossy magazine is the printed program with editorial material and advertising, all provided to the producers and theater owners for free by Playbill, Inc. It is a surprisingly big business.

Playbill is a monthly magazine that is customized for each performance venue and given to ticket holders of every Broadway show, many off-Broadway shows, and in theaters , both commercial and not-for-profit, in Boston; Chicago; Cincinnati; Columbus, Ohio; Dallas; Houston; Indianapolis; Miami; Minneapolis; Philadelphia; Phoenix; St. Louis; San Diego; San Francisco; and Washington, D.C. In addition one can subscribe or buy at a newsstand a generic monthly edition of *Playbill,* but the bulk of its circulation, just under four million copies per month, is given away in performance venues. This puts *Playbill* in the top 10 percent of monthly U.S. publications. Compare *Playbill's* circulation to *People Magazine* with a circulation of 3.6 million and *O, the Oprah Magazine* with circulation of 2.2 million. Playbill Inc. is a privately held company so it is not required by law to publish financial statements. Revenues are variously estimated to be $20 million to $37 million a year.

The theater audience, according to marketing surveys conducted by the Broadway League, is an attractive one for advertisers. The median household income of Broadway theatergoers was $148,000 in the 2007–8 season. The nationwide median household income was $50,300 in 2007, the most recent year for which U.S. Census figures are available. Before the show and at the intermission, audience members have time to read the program and experience the advertising. For some Broadway productions, especially long-lived musicals, producers sell a souvenir program: a full-color, photo-filled, large magazine-format book published on heavy-coated paper. Even in these cases, *Playbill* is still distributed free.

Playbill advertising is associated with a positive experience whereas advertising in magazines and newspapers may lie next to disturbing stories and photos. In addition many theatergoers keep their programs and share them with others so the advertisement gets even wider distribution. All this exposure can make advertising in *Playbill* attractive to the right companies. Recently *Playbill* has attracted advertisers such as high-end cosmetic manufacturers, Cadillac and Lexus automobiles, and legitimate pharmaceuticals aimed at seniors.

In the United States, the tradition of a free program for all attendees is well established, but this model is not followed in other countries. In London, for example, programs are designed and printed solely for a single show and are available only at a charge, recently as much as £3 or about $4.50 U.S. Not even simple cast lists and other artistic credits are available for free at most London commercial theaters. The National Theatre, however, often provides a free cast list.

Enhancing the *Playbill* brand is its Web site. Playbill.com offers theater news and information about ticket discounts. Theatrical souvenirs are for order. Playbill, Inc., also publishes cast albums and has an online radio stream, mostly of showtunes.

5

Ticket Pricing

Here's a way to pass some time on your next airline flight. Ask the folks seated around you how much they paid for their ticket. You might even make a bet on who paid the least. No one is surprised anymore that airline tickets for the same flight can be had for many different prices. Some customers may be puzzled by this fact. "Why is it so hard to know what a seat is worth?" they ask. Others think it's fun to try and get the lowest price. They study the patterns and have theories as to when is the best time to shop.

Pricing for theater tickets is also highly varied—unless the show is a standing-room-only hit and has no need to discount ticket prices. Similarly some airline flights are not discounted, if demand is high enough. It's not a good idea to talk while the show is going on, so just linger after the curtain comes down as the rest of the audience leaves and pick up ticket stubs from the floor. You'll find a number of different prices for seats in the same area of the theater. A *New York Times* article a few years ago found seven different ticket prices for orchestra seats at a single performance of the musical *Rent.*

Airlines and theaters use discounted pricing—called *price discrimination* or *yield management* or *demand-based pricing*—for the same reasons. Such pricing is also used by hotels and car rental agencies, again, for the same reasons, because in these businesses there is a particular relationship between revenues and costs, called *operating leverage,* and because the product they sell is perfectly perishable.

The easy one first: once a plane leaves the jetway, an empty seat is worthless. It cannot be stored up and sold on another day when more people want to fly. The same is true of an empty theater seat once the curtain goes up—worthless. A producer for *Rent* was quoted as saying that theater seats are like fruit, but he's wrong. Theater seats are far more perishable than fruit. Incidentally tickets that remain unsold after curtain time are called *deadwood* in the theater.

A Thought Experiment

Imagine it's 7:55 in the evening, and you approach a ticket office of a show that has unsold seats. You make an offer: "I'd like to see this show but not for $111.50. I'll give you $10 right now and take a seat. You'll have $10 more than you'll have otherwise. What do you say?" It's a tempting offer. Not only is the seat worthless in a few minutes; it costs the theater owner and producer *nothing extra* to put another bottom in a seat.

We'll return to the $10 offer in a bit, but this mention that there is no additional cost for selling one more ticket leads directly to the other reason that theaters sell tickets at many different prices: *high operating leverage.*

High Operating Leverage

The operating costs in the commercial theater do not change as more seats are sold. There may be a little more janitorial and accounting cost, but that's about it. Broadway theaters don't even pay for the programs they hand out, as mentioned earlier with *Playbill.* And the producer and theater owner may make a little money from an additional customer if he or she buys T-shirts, drinks, and snacks. Every seat sold is pure profit, once total revenue exceeds operating costs. This point, where the two lines of the chart in fig. 5.1 cross, is the *break-even point.* As a result, once a show meets break-even, profits mount quickly. On a weekly basis, the break-even revenue in the theater is called the *nut.*

Normal Operating Leverage for Comparison

But to understand the impact of this relationship in full, we need to look at a business with a more normal operating leverage. We could choose many businesses, but let's make it simple and examine a department store. A department store has some fixed costs—those that don't rise or fall with the volume of business—just to open the store: rent, energy, minimal staffing, and so on. Then, as the store makes each sale, costs rise. They rise primarily because if you buy a sweater, say, for fifty dollars, the store must pay the manufacturer for the wholesale cost of the sweater, typically 50 percent of the retail price, or, in this case, twenty-five dollars.

Revenues rise faster than costs, but there is still a break-even point, the point where costs and revenues are equal. This relationship is shown in figure 5.2. Unlike the scenario laid out in fig. 5.1, here, for a business with normal operating leverage, as revenues continue to rise after break-even, so do the operating costs. As a result profit does not rise as quickly for a business with normal operating leverage, such as our hypothetical department store, as it does for a business with high operating leverage, or, for our discussion, a commercial theater. Thus a business with normal operating leverage is less tempted to discount prices because the business has an additional cost for each unit sold.

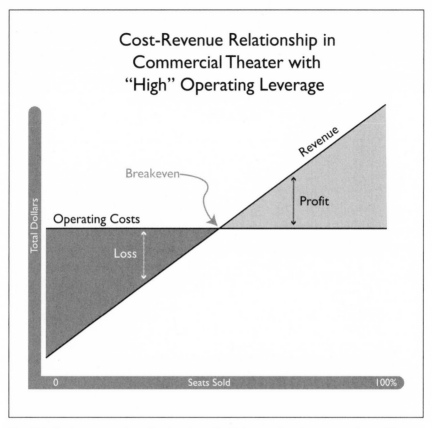

Fig. 5.1 Businesses such as the theater with high operating leverage make profit quickly or make losses quickly.

One might ask, wouldn't everyone want to be in a business with high operating leverage since the potential for profit is much greater? The problem is that the opposite is true as well. The potential for loss is greater, in equal proportion to the potential for profit. Compare the sides of the two charts to the left and right of the break-even point, figs. 5.1 and 5.2, and you'll see that, as you fail to make break-even, your losses in a business with high operating leverage will increase more quickly than in a business with normal operating leverage.

It's the general rule of economics presented earlier: greater profit only comes with greater risk. Despite what explanations show people consider when they lament the hit-or-flop nature of show business, a good part of the reason lies in the economic structure of commercial theater. High operating leverage increases both the potential for profit in good times and the risk of loss in lean times.

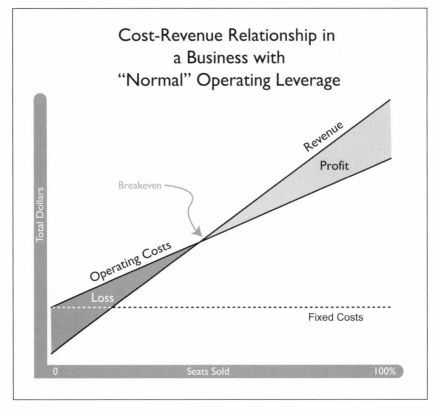

Fig. 5.2 A business with normal operating leverage has less risk than one with high operating leverage.

So it is with airlines. Airlines have shown high income volatility, in good part a result of high operating leverage. The first years of the twenty-first century have been bleak ones for the major airlines. Many companies went into bankruptcy and have emerged as smaller concerns than they were before this downturn began. Other companies have made defensive mergers, hoping their mutual weaknesses will result in a shared strength as one firm. There are many proximate reasons for the airlines' recent downturn: the aftermath of 9/11; the rise in fuel prices; competition from smaller, more financially nimble carriers. However, the business is inherently risky, and, when pressure comes from *any* source, losses can mount quickly.

In response to the recent stresses, airlines have downsized by reducing the number of flights. The result is that average occupancy per flight is higher. Higher occupancy makes the flight more profitable. And, for the public, flying is made more maddening than ever.

The Benefit of Inventory

Businesses with normal operating leverage typically make or sell a physical product, so they have inventory and that inventory is somewhat perishable but not perfectly perishable. The sweaters you looked at but didn't buy today can be folded, put back on the shelf, and, with luck, will sell another day. If not, they'll be marked down and eventually sold for some fraction of their original price. The store's buyer will order fewer goods for sale in slow months such as January and more goods for busy months such as December.

Increasing Revenue through Price Differentiation

Because a theater ticket is really a kind of rent on a seat, the commercial theater doesn't have the ability to manage its inventory of seats as the store manages its inventory of sweaters. But the commercial theater can manage *prices,* which leads us back to the thought experiment we started earlier: it's 7:55, and you offer the box office ten dollars for a seat right now.

The theater management is tempted, but it knows that, if it takes the ten dollars, word will get out. Soon the theater lobby will be crowded at curtain time with nervy people looking for a bargain. In addition to the problem of crowd control, the theater will start to lose money, as the discounted sales cannibalize the full-price ticket sales.

So *price differentiation* is a set of strategies to increase total revenues by offering discounts *with certain conditions,* so that people who are price sensitive are enticed to buy. Jeffrey Seller, a producer of *Rent* and *Avenue Q,* said, "We as an industry have priced at a level that is just too high for a lot of consumers who would like to go to the theater." The problem is to offer discounts to these price-sensitive customers without cannibalizing full-price sales so much that total revenues don't rise. Discounts come at a trade-off, often in convenience and choice. Compare the strategies of the airlines and the Broadway theater in price differentiation.

For the airlines the cheap seats come with many conditions, such as

- Some must be purchased four weeks in advance.
- There is no exchange or refund.
- Travel must include a Saturday night for some flights.
- There are a limited number of seats available at the discounted price, and the customer never knows how many are available and for which flight.

The cheapest seats for commercial theater are typically offered at the Theatre Development Fund ticket booth, called TKTS. The conditions at TKTS are

- Tickets are only available on the day of the performance.
- Some tickets must be bought with cash or travelers checks.

- There are limited ticket locations, at present in midtown New York, far downtown, and Brooklyn.
- There are usually long lines at the midtown site.
- Show and seat availability is limited, and the customer never knows for sure in advance what will be on sale.
- Seats are often less desirable, top balcony or to the sides of the theater.

The TKTS booth is useful for customers with time to stand in line, such as students and retirees. If you work during the day, TKTS is less convenient. If you need seats for a specific show because of a date or relatives visiting from out-of-town or you are visiting New York for a limited time, you will most likely buy full-price tickets. A big hit doesn't need to discount tickets, and so, usually, no tickets from hit shows are available at the TKTS site. Unless one is willing to wait until the demand for tickets for a hit show wanes and tickets become available at a discount, one pays full price. Wait for discounts, and you may miss seeing the performers who won the glowing reviews and the awards. These are some of the reasons the discounted tickets increase total revenues and do not totally cannibalize full-price ticket sales.

Theaters and theater producers have several means of price differentiation in addition to the TKTS booth. Shows send postcards with special code numbers entitling the user to receive a discount on tickets, bought in person at the box office or through the ticket agencies such as Telecharge and Ticketron, based on availability. Available good seats are not always discounted. Discount codes can be effective for producers particularly during the time a show is in previews, before reviews are out, to build audiences. In our Internet age, these code numbers are quickly spread, and now many discount codes are legitimately available on sites such as Playbill.com and BroadwayBox.com.

More traditional means of price differentiation include senior citizen discounts, reduced prices for lower demand performances such as Wednesday matinees, discount rates for group sales, and rush tickets. Note that rush tickets— a limited number of tickets sold shortly before curtain—have some of the characteristics of TKTS sales: waiting in line, uncertain availability, and often a cash-only sale. Many theater producers resisted these techniques, fearing that customers would be upset by the offers. For years the actors' union, Equity, was against increasing ticket prices for hit shows, arguing that "the average theater patron lives on a budget which allows just so much money for tickets to the theater . . . if that patron has to pay high prices . . . he is going to be able to go much less often." Price differentiation came in through the back door with the idea of offering day-of-performance discounted seats for shows that were not selling out. Now most producers are adapting many, or all, of the techniques of price differentiation.

The Impact of Price Differentiation

The bottom line is that price differentiation in the theater works. A 2005 study by a Stanford University economist examined tickets sales for the 199 performances of August Wilson's *Seven Guitars* in 1996. The producers of the play had designated seventeen different price levels for tickets. The economist applied a complex series of econometric models to the sales and estimated that price differentiation increased total revenues by 6 percent. For *Seven Guitars,* a play that grossed $4.34 million, price differentiation gave the producers more than $200,000 in revenue they wouldn't have had without the technique.

Price differentiation also potentially makes for a more diverse audience, since people from a greater range of economic circumstances can afford to attend if discount tickets are available. For some producers or some plays, expanding audience diversity can be an important goal of price setting.

What Happened to Scaling the House?

Once mezzanine seats were cheaper than orchestra seats. And balcony seats were cheaper yet. The practice of pricing seats based on the attractiveness of their location is called *scaling the house.* But there is generally less scaling today as demand pricing has taken hold. For one example, look at fig. 5.3, the seating chart for the Shubert Theatre in the summer of 2007, where *Spamalot* was playing; during that period *Spamalot* was a smash hit. We chose the Shubert for no particular reason; we could have chosen most any commercial Broadway house with about the same result. All but the last two rows of the mezzanine were priced at the same level as the orchestra. In fact even partial view seats in the orchestra and mezzanine were priced at the highest price—$116.50 on a weekend night.

For comparison a show at the Shubert from the mid-1960s was picked essentially at random. The British-import musical *Stop the World, I Want to Get Off* was a strong hit. The highest price was an orchestra ticket. The mezzanine had three prices: 80 percent, 67 percent, and 56 percent of the highest price. The balcony had two prices, 42 percent and 33 percent of the highest price. Incidentally the highest-price ticket for *Stop the World* was $8.60. Based on the consumer price index, that would be $57.30 in 2006 dollars. Orchestra seats for *Spamalot* in the summer of 2007 were $111.50 to $116.50.

Premium Seats: The Opposite of Discounts

But the list price of orchestra seats for *Spamalot* was not the highest price available from the box office. That price was for the so-called *premium seats,* selling for anywhere from $176.50 to $251.50. Where are the premium seats? No one but the producer and the theater owner knows, and they won't tell. How many premium seats are available? No one but the producer and the theater owner knows, and they won't tell. The practice of offering premium seats began in October 2001, when the

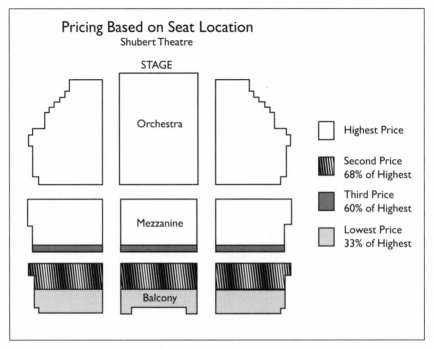

Fig. 5.3 The Shubert Theatre seating chart for *Spamalot* offers few seats at less than the highest price. However, if any show doesn't sell all its tickets, the show's producers will likely offer some tickets through discount sources, such as the TKTS booths.

producers of *The Producers,* after receiving rave reviews, decided to beat ticket scalpers at their own game. The theater reserved some number of quality seats— proverbially described as "eighth row center" but actually about one hundred seats a night—to be sold at a premium price. Typically, a week before the performance, one-half of the unsold premium seats are released for general sale; two days before, the remaining premium seats are halved again and then again on the day of the show. Talk about pricing based on demand! This is why, when you get a last-minute seat for a nearly sold-out show, it can be a very good seat. The moral: no show is ever sold out. Never give up.

One producer of *The Producers* said that, if people were willing to pay so much for good seats to ticket scalpers, then it was only fair that the investors, producers, and the creative team behind the production should be the ones making the money. This rhetoric seems to have persuaded the theatergoing audience that premium seats are a legitimate tactic and not price gouging.

Now the Broadway theaters have demand-based pricing in *both* directions: lower prices for shows that have unsold seats and higher prices for standing-room-only hits. During the summer of 2007, the *average* ticket price for the hit jukebox musical *Jersey Boys* was about $122 as reported in *Variety*. But the *highest list price* for a ticket to *Jersey Boys* was $111.50. The sale of a number of premium tickets made up the difference. Premium tickets to *Jersey Boys* were $302 or even $352, and enough people bought them to make *Jersey Boys*' average ticket price higher than the highest list price. According to Shubert Organization CEO Philip J. Smith, premium tickets can add as much as "$100,000 a week to the gross, if you've got a hot musical. A hot play, could be $50,000." Over all Paul Lubin, Jujamcyn's producing director, believes premium price tickets have increased Broadway revenues by at least 10 percent.

Scalping Laws Scrapped

Premium ticket pricing may be only the beginning. On March 19, 2007, Gerald Schoenfeld, then chairman of the Broadway League and chairman of the Shubert Foundation, testified to the New York State Consumer Protection Board in favor of dismantling the antiscalping laws, which limit the resale of tickets. Under the

The TKTS Booth

TKTS opened in 1973. At TKTS, tickets are usually offered at a 50 percent discount with an additional four-dollar fee to support the Theatre Development Fund. In the spring of 2009, the Broadway League quietly added a one-dollar fee to TKTS tickets. The league expects to net about $1 million a year to use for marketing the Broadway brand. There are three locations: midtown Manhattan on Duffy Square, in the South Street Seaport in Lower Manhattan, and downtown Brooklyn. The Duffy Square site was first established as a temporary structure using trailers. Finally a permanent TKTS building on the square was opened late in 2008. Available shows are displayed on large digital signs near the ticket windows.

The impact of the half-price booth is substantial. In a typical week, TKTS sells $2 million in tickets to Broadway and off-Broadway shows. More than 7 percent of Broadway tickets are sold through the half-price booth. The TKTS formula is effective and is used in other U.S. and European cities.

The Theatre Development Fund, a not-for-profit service organization for the performing arts, was founded in 1968. Its initial focus was to subsidize tickets for secondary-school students. Now it has many additional activities, which include supporting sign-language interpretation in theaters, providing workshops for secondary school students, maintaining a costume collection, and recognizing theater professionals with several award programs.

law at that time, licensed ticket resellers could charge no more than 20 percent over the list price of a Broadway ticket. The assumption of interested followers of the theater is that the Broadway League producers want to set up Internet bidding sites for the most desirable tickets to hit shows. On June 1, 2007, the New York state law against scalping was allowed to expire.

Although the producers are not auctioning tickets over the Internet, existing Internet resellers of theater, concert, and sport tickets are emboldened. At least one such ticket-resale Web site, *Stubhub.com,* opened a store on 40th Street near Broadway. To be fair, according to a Stubhub.com spokesman, by far most of the tickets they resell are for concerts and sports events, with few seats available for Broadway shows.

With this change the revolution to pricing theater tickets by demand is complete. The hits will make even more money. There's nothing wrong with that. But in all likelihood some producers may budget their shows in ways that work only if the shows sell premium tickets. If they do so, the hit-or-flop nature of the commercial theater will escalate.

Ticket prices for live performances or entertainment in New York City tend to cluster between about $50 and $130, with some notable exceptions, as fig. 5.4 shows.

Not-for-Profit Ticket Prices

The not-for-profit theater also uses price differentiation to maximize ticket revenue. Just like the commercial theater, the not-for-profit theater has a perfectly perishable product: an unsold seat is worthless once the performance begins.

However, because much of the not-for-profit theater's fixed costs are met by subscriptions and by contributed income, also known as donations, it is sheltered from a good deal of risk. Fig. 5.5 resembles the cost-revenue chart of the high operating·leverage commercial theater that was shown earlier in fig. 5.1, but revenue doesn't start at zero for the not-for-profit theaters. Furthermore, by definition there is no profit for a not-for-profit. The not-for-profit word for revenue in excess of cost is *surplus.*

Ticket Price and Inflation

Average ticket prices on Broadway have increased faster than the rate of inflation as measured by the consumer price index (CPI) for the New York City area. Fig. 5.6 compares actual average ticket price to what the average price would have been if, starting in the 1985 season, the price increased by the New York City area CPI. The actual average ticket price in 2006 was just under $72. If ticket prices had risen at the same rate as inflation for these 21 years, the ticket price would have been only $57.80.

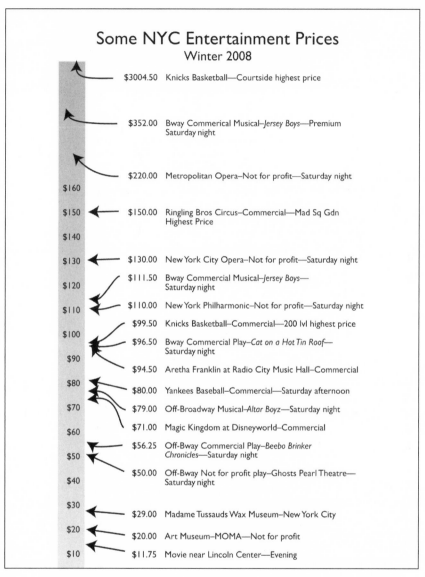

Some NYC Entertainment Prices
Winter 2008

$3004.50 — Knicks Basketball—Courtside highest price

$352.00 — Bway Commerical Musical–*Jersey Boys*—Premium Saturday night

$220.00 — Metropolitan Opera–Not for profit—Saturday night

$160

$150 ← $150.00 — Ringling Bros Circus–Commercial—Mad Sq Gdn Highest Price

$140

$130 ← $130.00 — New York City Opera–Not for profit—Saturday night

$120 — $111.50 — Bway Commercial Musical–*Jersey Boys*—Saturday night

$110 — $110.00 — New York Philharmonic–Not for profit—Saturday night

$99.50 — Knicks Basketball–Commercial—200 lvl highest price

$100 — $96.50 — Bway Commercial Play–*Cat on a Hot Tin Roof*—Saturday night

$90 — $94.50 — Aretha Franklin at Radio City Music Hall–Commercial

$80 — $80.00 — Yankees Baseball–Commercial—Saturday afternoon

$70 — $79.00 — Off-Broadway Musical–*Altar Boyz*—Saturday night

$60 — $71.00 — Magic Kingdom at Disneyworld–Commercial

$56.25 — Off-Bway Commercial Play–*Beebo Brinker Chronicles*—Saturday night

$50 — $50.00 — Off-Bway Not for profit play–Ghosts Pearl Theatre—Saturday night

$40

$30 ← $29.00 — Madame Tussauds Wax Museum–New York City

$20 ← $20.00 — Art Museum–MOMA—Not for profit

$10 ← $11.75 — Movie near Lincoln Center—Evening

Fig. 5.4 Entertainment prices in New York City tend to cluster from $50 to $130.

Interestingly, in the 1987 through 1991 seasons, average ticket prices rose at a rate *less* than inflation. As much as producers, like any business people, would like to control the market price for their goods, there are times when the market says no. There was not a broad choice of enticing material on Broadway in the period from 1987 to 1991 according to most observers. The rise in average ticket price

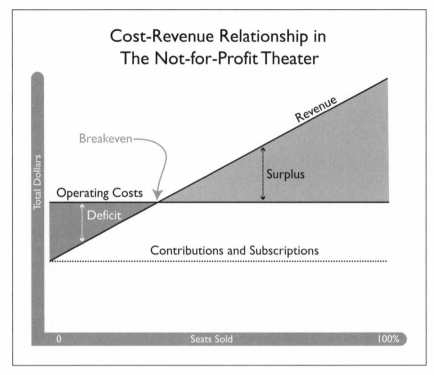

Fig. 5.5 Contributed income and subscriptions cover a large part of the not-for-profit theater's operating costs.

may reflect this observation. Yes, this period saw the premiere of some Broadway powerhouse musicals, including *The Phantom of the Opera, Les Misérables,* and *Miss Saigon.* Yet in this period Tony Award nominations for best musical were given for such forgettable shows—flops—as *Big Deal, Rags, Starmites, Aspects of Love,* and *Starlight Express* because they were the only shows available to nominate. There was not much exceptional product to draw audiences to Broadway at this time, so average ticket prices could not rise quickly.

The Economic Dilemma of the Performing Arts

One reason that ticket prices for theater and all performing arts are rising faster than inflation was definitively described by economists W. J. Baumol and W. G. Bowen in 1966: the effect is called the *economic dilemma of the performing arts.* The crux is *productivity.* Little opportunity presents itself for increasing productivity in the performing arts. A string quartet takes four musicians now as it did for Haydn in the late eighteenth century; "The Minute Waltz" always takes a minute to play, more or less. Some lesser roles in Shakespeare plays can be doubled, played by a

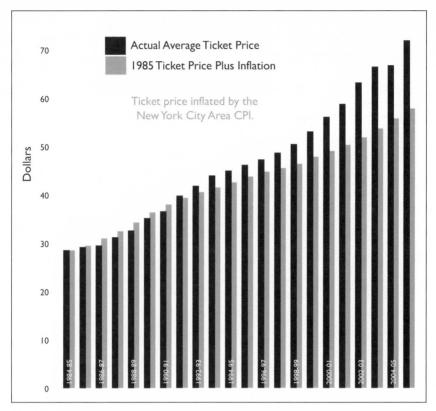

Fig. 5.6 Starting with the 1991 season, Broadway ticket prices rose faster than inflation.

single actor in different dress—Shakespeare's theater did so—but only to a point.

Meanwhile most industries are constantly using techniques, machinery, economies of scale, and new technology to increase productivity, which allows businesses to afford to raise employee salaries to keep pace with the general inflation of modern times. Although economists may argue about how productivity is defined, for purposes of this discussion a simple definition suffices: productivity is a measure of the output per hour of labor. Annual average nonfarm productivity in the period from 2000 through 2007 increased 2.5 percent per year.

How can the theater increase productivity? Offer more than eight performances a week with the same cast, working for the same salary. Stage smaller-cast plays, using only a single set. Replace some actors or musicians with mechanical simulacra. Increase the numbers of seats in the theater. With the exception of the union rule of eight shows a week, most of these tactics have been used to some extent. Even the union rule of maximum weekly performances was modified by Equity to accommodate the short run of the seasonal musical *Irving Berlin's White*

Christmas. This stage adaptation of the holiday movie musical played the Marquis Theatre November 14, 2008, through January 4, 2009, with nine shows some weeks. Even with added performances, *Irving Berlin's White Christmas,* with more than thirty actors and twenty-four musicians, needed to play on average to audiences of at least 90 percent of capacity and gross $10.5 million total to recoup a $4 million capitalization in just seven-and-a-half weeks.

With increasing frequency new plays have limited numbers of actors and limited scenery. Large cast nonmusical plays are almost unaffordable, commercially or by most not-for-profit theaters. The extreme example of the shrinking cast is the one-person show. Musicians are being replaced with synthetic computer-driven music sources, with product names such as Notion and Sinfonia. Understandably the musicians' union fights all such innovations. The biggest Broadway theaters are the newest ones, and the performing arts centers where many touring companies perform are bigger still. Yet there comes a limit to how big a theater can become before the sensation of a live experience is lost.

Even actors must eat, and so the payment to performers and others in the theater must generally rise as inflation rises. Costs of advertising, rent, and matériel are advancing as well. Since the performing arts have no way to increase productivity, the price of tickets must rise faster than inflation since the costs of inputs to performances continually grow.

This inescapable structural problem is in large part the underlying economic motive for the growth in importance of the not-for-profit theater. It takes subsidies and donations to keep ticket prices affordable to a broader range of people. One suspects the trend to not-for-profit organizations for theater can only increase. And the percentage of not-for-profit budgets that comes from contributions versus what comes from ticket sales will also increase. Either this, or ticket prices will continue to rise, making professional theater even more inaccessible to people of limited means.

Easy Prediction: Ticket Prices Will Rise

Theater is structured like other businesses and so finds it advantageous to adopt some of the same modern techniques developed for other businesses. Improved marketing, such as using the Internet for promotion and ticket sales, and, most important, demand-based pricing are some such techniques. Even with these advances, theater is affected by the economic dilemma of the performing arts, an inability to increase productivity. As long as producers and artistic directors find attractive plays, musicals, performers, and productions, the price of theater tickets will rise, and audiences will pay.

Intermission

The Glut of Performers—
Actors' Earnings and Actors Equity Association

Most actors cannot make a living through their craft and art alone. To put it simply, there are too many actors chasing too few paying roles. And the actors' union is shaped by the economic challenges its members face.

In economic terms there is an *overcapacity* of actors, *an economic glut.* There are more actors than the market—producers, not-for-profit theaters, and whoever else—cares to buy. In search of jobs, actors accept less and less money, until they find work. Sometimes actors act for no money at all. When overcapacity happens to a commodity, such as corn or wheat, in the next season fewer farmers grow the commodity that is in glut and a more sustainable price establishes itself. With actors this self-correction doesn't seem to work, and so the average actor's wages are consistently lower than the average for the American workforce.

Actors' Earnings

"Hi-diddle-dee-dee / An actor's life for me" sings Jiminy Cricket in the 1940 Disney animated classic *Pinocchio.* "A high silk hat and a silver cane / A watch of gold with a diamond chain."

Popular media today paints a similarly glittering vision of the life of actors who are *stars,* that very small percentage of performers whose irreproducible qualities —physical beauty, training, talent, creativity, psychological availability, luck, and a good press agent—enable them to lead lives that are financially rich. The financial life of the average actor is nothing of the sort. It's a very old joke: needing service in a busy Manhattan restaurant, someone shouts, "Actor!" All the waiters turn to the voice. Waiting tables, temping at legal offices, cat-sitting—actors work as they can between stage jobs.

At least Actors Equity Association (Equity) is honest about it. Each year the union of actors and stage managers publishes a season report, an analysis of

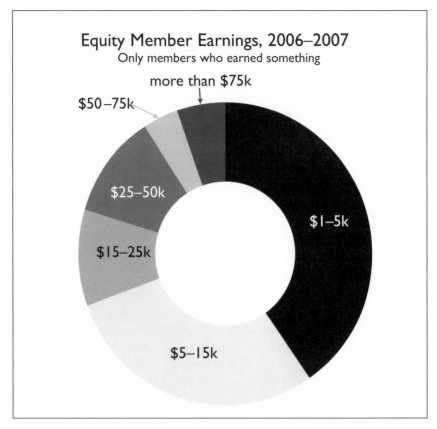

Fig. I.1 Of Equity members who earned anything in 2007, 21 percent earned
$25,000 or more. This chart is redrawn from one in the Equity annual report.

employment and earnings. It's sobering reading. There's little change over time;
the figures used here come from the 2006–7 season report. Equity membership
totals 41,358, but for this season fewer than 18,000 worked in the profession *at all*.
Only 43 percent of members worked as an actor or stage manager over the entire
season; during an average week, just over 14 percent worked in their trade. Average weeks worked per member was a mere 17. Median member earnings from acting or stage managing were a little more than seven thousand dollars a year.

This is the status of those who are clearly professional actors, members of the
professional union. What sort of living nonunion actors make is hard to determine. There are some hints. The NEA produced a report on artists in the workforce using census figures. The census figures are useful but not perfect, given the
way the census defined professional actor.

How many working actors are there in the United States? The 2000 census,
lumping together stage, film, and television actors, union and nonunion, claims

39,717. This figure should give one pause. Actors Equity has more than 40,000 members alone. Then there are the working, nonunion stage actors of unknown numbers across the United States. The Screen Actors Guild (SAG), which represents "working actors in film, television, industrials, commercials, video games, music videos, and other new media" claims more than 120,000 members.

The census figure is probably accurate given how the census did its work. People were surveyed and were assigned the profession in which they *worked the most hours in the week before the census interview.* We know from Equity's annual reports that only 17 percent of its members work in any average week. One reliable source claims that as many as 30,000 SAG actors don't find work in any given year.

One might also be tempted to question the survey when noticing that the third-ranking community in the United States by working actors as a percent of population is Medford-Ashland, Oregon, a town of 21,000 full-year population. However, if one knows that Ashland is home to the Oregon Shakespeare Festival,

Fig. I.2 This is the same graph as found on p. 96 redrawn to include the Equity members who had no earnings from acting.

which hires 325 full-time and 175 part-time staff, the ranking makes sense. If the census came to Ashland in the period that the Oregon Shakespeare Festival is dark, November through mid-February, Ashland wouldn't rank in the top thousand. The census has an element of chance in it, or better put, an element of probability.

So the census isn't everything one might want, but its figures are the broadest statistics that are available. Actors in the census have a median age of 35. This makes them younger than the civilian labor force, whose median is 40 years. Forty-five percent of the actors are female, which is comparable to the labor force as a whole, and 23 percent are part of a minority, somewhat lower than the labor force at 30 percent. Actors have attained much higher educational levels than the labor force as a whole. More than 58 percent have a bachelor's degree or higher, compared to less than 28 percent for the labor force as a whole.

The median yearly income for actors from all sources was $23,400; for the civilian labor force, it was $30,100. About 61 percent of the civilian workforce was employed full-year, full-time; for actors it was just over 15 percent. For those working full-year, full-time, median income was $38,700 for the workforce; only $31,500 for actors.

Actors sacrifice financially to pursue their art. Actors receive less income from all sources than an average worker with comparable education and training would receive. Some economists refer to this gap as *discounted labor*. By remaining actors, these individuals are contributing to the bottom line of theaters by earning less than they could in other professions. Except for being somewhat involuntary, the contribution is not totally unlike that of governments, foundations, corporations, and individuals who make donations to the theater. As an actor said in a meeting of the National Congress of Actors and Acting Teachers, "We are subsidizing the theater." Contrast that with a response that is either more positive—or totally ironic—from another actor at the same conference, who said, as an actor, "You can explore the depths of your soul. That is your pay."

Even in New York City, the center of stage acting in the United States, actors will perform for nothing and compete to get the job. One example is the Flea Theatre, a ninety-nine-seat off-off-Broadway theater in a converted factory in lower Manhattan, which calls its company of actors the Bats. Why the name? Because one of the founders of the theater remarked that a person would have to be bats to work off-off-Broadway. Twice a year, when the Flea auditions for a new company, close to one thousand applicants compete, all nonunion. For those chosen to be Bats, the pay is zero. Moreover, each Bat must log five hours of work each week in addition to any acting or rehearsal, doing jobs such as stuffing envelopes, serving drinks in the bar, or painting and cleaning the building. The Flea is upfront about the requirements. An information sheet given to auditionees states, "The main problem with the company is that the work is intense and can be enormously time consuming." The Flea Theatre budget in 2006 was just under seven hundred thousand dollars. Its mission is "to present edgy and distinctive work that raises the standards of Off-Off-Broadway for artists and audiences alike. . . . Each year The Flea presents and produces dozens of new works in an environment that is professional, welcoming, and intimate." The Flea has received two OBIE Awards, the distinguished award for off-Broadway and off-off-Broadway work given by the weekly newspaper the *Village Voice.* It also has received a Drama Desk Award for Distinguished Achievement.

The problem of maintaining a living wage continues for actors living outside of New York City. While no organization reports specifically for this group, there are anecdotal reports. In 2007 the *Chicago Tribune* wrote about the earnings prospects of Chicagoland actors. The large Chicago theaters, members of the League of Resident Theatres (LORT), have Equity contracts and offer standard union pay for LORT theaters, ranging in 2008 from $544 to $840 per week minimum, depending on the theater size. The three Chicago LORT theaters are the Goodman, the Court, and Northlight. Not many actors, even at LORT theaters, work full-year, full-time. If actors work at least twenty weeks out of the year, they are eligible for health insurance from Equity, an important consideration.

Members of the Producers of Chicago Area Theatres, or PCAT, have a separately negotiated contract with Equity. That contract covers about fifty producers and allows the producers to hire Equity and non-Equity actors under certain rules and proportions. PCAT union salary minimums in 2008 ranged from $162.50 to $700 weekly, depending on the potential box office gross of the venue. Nonunion actors make less at the PCAT theaters and at Chicago-area theaters without Equity agreements. Some nonunion companies offer actors a one-time stipend ranging from $25 to $500, according to the *Chicago Tribune* report. Others offer no money or up to $200 per week. Incidentally, and contrary to myth, the *Tribune* avers that the job of choice among actors is not waiting tables but a day job in an office with health insurance.

The *Denver Post* in 2006 reported the dilemma of union membership for Colorado actors. Equity membership offers more pay and the chance of working enough weeks to qualify for health insurance. But, out of Colorado's ninety-four theater companies, only eight were Equity theaters at the time. Only the Denver Center Theatre Company is a member of LORT. Its minimum salary was $725 a week. By contrast, another Colorado Equity theater, the Aurora Fox, which is not a LORT theater, must hire at least two Equity actors per show. The Fox pays an Equity actor $177 per week plus pension and health benefits payments and a non-Equity actor $150 per week. Not much more than lunch money and carfare.

It must be noted that actors are not the only theater artists that have a hard time making a living at their trade. Itinerant directors and designers are similarly challenged. Some of the union minimums may seem adequate in themselves, but these theater artists are limited in the number of jobs they can attract and perform in a year. One Los Angeles–based theater director said, "In my very best year, I made just over $55,000. And I practically killed myself to do it." The minimum payment of the Stage Directors and Choreographers Society (SDC) to a director in a LORT theater ranges from $6,344 for no more than four weeks and three days' rehearsal in the lowest-scaled LORT house, called LORT D, to $24,000 for five weeks and two days in the highest-scaled house, LORT A+. In some of the smaller not-for-profit professional theaters, SDC rates can be as low as $1,943 for an eight-day rehearsal period at a resident stock company or $988 at a dinner theater. Itinerant union designers face similar economic obstacles in making a living.

Douglas Hughes, director of the not-for-profit play and hit Broadway transfer *Doubt* and a resident director of the Roundabout Theatre, commented that, as an artistic director of a not-for-profit theater, "I found myself continually reminding the theater's board that the operation of their theater was heavily subsidized by the artists who made work on their stages. . . . A very good year [for a director] made up of a combination of four or five LORT contracts harvests less than forty thousand dollars. Three LORT D productions earn a far-below-poverty-level thirteen thousand dollars."

Inevitably the question arises: why do actors and other theater artists do it—why not pick a more comfortable career? A definitive answer to this question is beyond the scope of this book. The happiest thought is that actors are driven by artistic ambition. With the many sacrifices necessary to continue to be an actor, the most honest way to refer to the actors' craft is as a *vocation:* a calling, a response to a compelling inner need. The term *vocation* is borrowed from the world of religious orders.

All artists, whether poets, painters, or potters, face a hard row to reach financial security from their art. And no one sets out to be just average, no matter what the profession. The typical business majors in college don't know the average earnings for their profession—nor do they plan to earn only that much. For actors there is, perhaps, the appeal of gambling: betting on getting a role through the frustration of auditioning, hoping for the long shot to wind up among the tiny percentage of performers who become stars. Gambling can be a powerful addiction.

Maybe it's just that acting looks *easy.* Here's an analogy to music. Put an untrained person behind a drum set, and he or she thinks, "I'm a drummer!" Put this untrained individual at a piano keyboard, and the result is "I'm not a pianist." This is why, as a musician friend puts it, "there are so many drummers and so little time." In music, *time* is a synonym for meter or rhythm.

From the audience's point of view, an actor's art seems effortless and spontaneous. Maybe this seeming easiness is part of the attraction to would-be actors.

Surely no one without training and experience as a tailor or seamstress would undertake to design, cut, sew, and tailor, for example, a pink woman's suit that must look fresh out of the tissue paper from the Chanel atelier—a necessary outfit for a production of Wendy Wasserstein's *The Sisters Rosensweig.* Everyone knows there is technique and craft to costume design and construction. But many potential actors would audition for any part in that or any other play for which they are age and gender appropriate, whether or not they have the training and talent to act the part.

It seems that time corrects the employment problem for many individual actors. Being a journeyman actor is a young person's game. As people age, many accept less than their artistic ideal, trading ambition for a steady job as a non-artist, a family, health insurance, the hope of a funded retirement. They settle and settle down. Maybe that's why the actors surveyed by the census are younger on average than the workforce as a whole.

Actors Equity Association

Equity has a grand founding story, but it has grown into an unusual labor organization. Most established labor groups want more members to increase the organization's reach and power. Equity works to *limit* members of its union. At heart is the problem this chapter started with: too many actors for too few roles.

In the late nineteenth and early twentieth centuries, when much of theater work was in touring from town to town, touring was dominated by an alliance called the Theatre Syndicate. The syndicate was in essence a monopoly and could blackball any performer who dared to disagree with its rules. Rehearsals could be any length of time and for no pay. Actors were paid only for performances. Actors supplied and maintained their own costumes. Backstage spaces were usually dirty, unheated or sweltering, often with no running water and thus no toilets. Productions could close without notice, leaving the actors stranded without pay or transportation home. Producer Jed Harris is quoted on the Actors Equity Association Web site describing the era before Equity was established: "It was dog eat dog and vice versa."

Actors Equity Association was formed in 1913 to address these and other issues of actors. Equity continues to focus very well on issues of health and safety. The stage of a modern Broadway musical can be a dangerous place, with computer-controlled, mechanized scenery and trapdoors; deafening music and sound effects; moving light fixtures; and theatrical smoke and fog. Actors need Equity as much as ever. Equity has also worked for pension funds and health insurance for its members and salary increases over time. But Equity's power is limited by the overcapacity of actors. In response Equity has tried to function as a *closed shop,* a business where employees can be hired only from the union rolls.

Closed shops were effective in enabling collective bargaining in instances where employers were many and they often changed names and moved headquarters. Such employers include the construction business and the commercial theater. Closed shops were powerful tools of union leaders in cementing control of the union; dissident or competing members could be discharged from the union, and, once discharged from the union, they lost their jobs. Members owed their jobs and so their allegiance to the union, not to their employer.

In 1947 the Taft-Hartley Act outlawed the closed shop. A *union shop* is legal: one in which employees are required to join unions or at least pay union dues and in which expulsion from the union is not sufficient reason to lose a job. However, the National Labor Relations Board (NLRB) has some discretion to enter into agreements in special situations. Equity is one of these situations. To join Equity, one must be hired to work in a union production or be a member of Equity's sister unions: the Screen Actors Guild, the American Federation of Television and Radio Artists, or some smaller unions. In addition students can work for membership by receiving fifty weeks' credit for work in an Equity theater and paying a four hundred–dollar fee with application.

For many years, however, Equity's arrangement with commercial producers forbade the producers from auditioning non-Equity actors. In 1987, in response to a nonunion actor filing charges with the NLRB, Equity created a new level of affiliation with the union, eligibility status. For a nominal annual fee, nonunion actors who met experience and salary minimums could purchase a card permitting them access to Equity auditions. Though the agreement seemed to open up the process, over time Equity raised the criteria, making eligibility status not greatly different from membership.

In 1997 the NLRB let Equity dismantle the eligibility status system. Instead Equity's agreements with producers would require the producers to hold non-Equity auditions. The non-Equity auditions would be after the Equity auditions, but their duration and format were unspecified, and they were not policed by Equity, the NLRB, or anyone else.

Equity is not gaining power over its membership by running the equivalent of a closed shop; rather Equity's members demand that the union work on the problem of unemployment and underemployment of its members. To protect its members, Equity tries to limit access to union jobs.

Still, Equity is in a symbiotic relationship with the commercial producers and not-for-profit theater directors who hire its members. Equity cannot push too hard for salary increases for fear of undermining the financial security of the not-for-profit theaters or influencing commercial producers to use nonunion actors where they can, such as on tour. One example of the interrelation of Equity and the not-for-profit theater is the status of *protected theater.* Not-for-profit theaters that run deficits are put in protected status, which reduces the minimum payments they must make as salary and benefit payments.

Whatever strength Equity has comes from a couple of the union's unusual qualities. Equity is blessed to be connected to the commercial Broadway theater, where virtually all employees are union. Usually a strike by one of the entertainment unions is recognized by all of them. Moreover, labor disputes in the entertainment industry have an enormous public impact. Stage artists have easy access to the channels of publicity. Producers know they are in an image business and avoid being associated with unattractive events, such as labor actions. Producers cannot hire replacement workers, or scabs, to continue work during a strike. Equity's power, such as it is, did not erode in the last half of the twentieth century, when the strength of most American labor unions was in decline. Union membership in the United States was about a third of the workforce a half century ago. By 2005 only 12.5 percent of U.S. workers were members of a union.

As described earlier, the performing arts have a productivity problem, which means that the costs of producing all the performing arts, including theater, rise faster than the general rate of inflation. To some extent this is mitigated by the perception of the theater as a luxury good, worth more than substitutes such as television or the movies. *Luxury good* is a term in economics for goods for which a rise in price will create increased revenue for the manufacturers. This term contrasts with *necessity goods,* for which a price rise normally reduces demand so much that total revenue does not increase, at least for a while. Still, pressure remains to hold down the earnings of theater artists, no matter what their unions do. As long as there are so many potential actors—and directors and designers—with the drive to practice their art, their average earnings will remain meager.

The Not-for-Profit Professional Theater

Not-for-profit theaters usually begin with the artists' need for expression. Few begin with a business plan. Yet the not-for-profit theaters that thrive become businesses nonetheless. They need money management, marketing, personnel, janitorial services, heating and cooling, legal services, and so on. As businesses, not-for-profit theaters move through the well-established business life cycle, if they survive and grow. The movement from the enthusiasm of a few to the organization of many others is a story worth telling.

It is reasonably certain that the not-for-profit theater in the United States had total budgets in the 2005–6 season of $1.79 billion. This figure comes from 990 reports that the IRS requires each not-for-profit corporation to file. This total revenue is roughly equivalent to the total revenues of all the Broadway League productions, both Broadway and touring, $1.9 billion in the 2006–7 season. The problem is figuring what portion of the $1.79 billion is for *professional* not-for-profit theater. For there is no consistently accepted and applied definition of a professional theater.

The Not-For-Profit Professional Theater Definition Examined

The *not-for-profit* part is easy to define. To qualify as a not-for-profit, an operation must receive the 501(c)3 designation from the Internal Revenue Service. Donations to 501(c)3 organizations are tax deductible, and 501(c)3 organizations are mostly tax exempt. The IRS 501(c)3 exemption applies to incorporated organizations operated exclusively for "religious, charitable, scientific, testing for public safety, literary, or educational purposes, or to foster national or international amateur sports competition, or for the prevention of cruelty to children or animals." Theaters are called "private operating foundations," not-for-profit organizations that use most earnings and assets directly for tax-exempt purposes, rather than making grants to others. There are more than a million 501(c)3 corporations in the United States, although some of these may no longer be active concerns. The 501(c)3 theaters annual Form 990 reports are publicly available, making much information about these outfits accessible. As already noted, the total budgets for not-for-profit theaters in 2005–6 was $1.79 billion. There were 1,893 not-for-profit theaters reporting to the IRS in that year.

The problem is identifying professional not-for-profit theaters. There are theaters that clearly define themselves as amateur, although they have some paid personnel, and, at the other end of the spectrum, theaters that engage solely union actors and other union personnel and thus are clearly professional. Between those extremes a clear meaning of "professional" is unclear.

Size is not enough to differentiate the professional and not-for-profit theaters. In the authors' hometown, for instance, each of the two dominant community theaters has a budget greater than the budget of the one professional not-for-profit theater, based on recent IRS 990 reports. The amateur theaters pay salaries and fees to some participants: artistic or executive directors, box office and some other financial staff, directors and designers and technicians, and musicians when producing musicals. Actors are never paid, and many positions in these theaters are filled by unpaid volunteers. In this mix of employees and volunteers the amateur community theaters in the authors' hometown are typical of not-for-profit amateur theaters in the United States.

The professional theater in our hometown pays actors—but far below a living wage—and many other professional staff but also relies upon volunteers. This theater is different from the two community theaters in that it *defines itself* as professional and that it is a member of the dominant trade organization for professional not-for-profit theaters, Theatre Communications Group (TCG).

A commonsense definition of a professional would be someone who earns a living from a specified activity. A weekend sandlot softball player is an amateur. He or she plays for the love of the sport; the Latin for the word *love* is embedded in the word *amateur.* For a contrasting example, consider Joe Blanton, a pitcher for the Philadelphia Phillies; he is a *professional,* said to earn more than $3 million a year. The actors for many not-for-profit professional theaters do not make a living wage. Even union membership is not enough to guarantee a living wage from theater. As noted previously, Equity salaries for Chicago Area Theatres, a contract group under Equity, can be as little as $162.50 a week. A living wage for Chicago is estimated to be $243.60 per week, according to federal government statistics. Furthermore, because members of the union insisted, now Equity even endorses actors appearing in off-off-Broadway showcases under specific limits for a payment that is essentially subway fare. Outside the actors' union, there are other professional associations that may help provide definitions of professional theater through their membership requirements.

Theatre Communications Group

The Theatre Communications Group is the dominant trade organization representing professional not-for-profit theater. TCG's mission is "to strengthen, nurture and promote the professional not-for-profit American theater." It was founded in 1961 through a multiyear Ford Foundation grant intended to create a entity that would gather and disseminate information about the professional not-for-profit theater in the United States. TCG publishes the monthly magazine *American Theatre* with a circulation of around twenty-one thousand copies. TCG is also the leading publisher of trade editions of new plays in America.

To be eligible to join TCG, theaters must, among other things, have a budget of at least fifty thousand dollars, rehearsals of at least thirty hours per production, professional paid leadership, and payment to actors equivalent to the Equity minimum for the area *or* at least 20 percent of the theater's annual budget dedicated to artist compensation. A not-for-profit theater can reach 20 percent of its budget by paying artist compensation to artistic directors, directors, and designers with little or nothing to actors. TCG has more than four hundred member theaters in forty-seven states. But TCG is not the only organization representing not-for-profit professional theaters.

The League of Resident Theatres

The League of Resident Theatres (LORT) was founded to promote the general welfare of professional resident theaters in the United States, to encourage relations among resident theaters, to provide resident theaters with opportunities to act in their common interests, and to represent its members in labor relations. LORT has seventy-seven active members in twenty-nine states and the District of Columbia (see fig. 6.1.)

The term *resident theater* is largely anachronistic. It originally described a theater with a company of actors presenting a season of plays or a rolling repertory of plays; the acting company was *resident* during the season. Few year-round, not-for-profit theaters work on this model now. Instead they engage actors for a single play. Summer festivals, often focused on large cast shows such as those of Shakespeare and often located in small, picturesque towns, may still accurately be called resident theaters. In any case the term stuck for the entire class of not-for-profit professional theaters.

LORT membership requirements are clear:

- The theater must be incorporated as a non-profit IRS-approved organization.
- Each self-produced production must be rehearsed for a minimum of three weeks.
- The theater must have a playing season of twelve weeks or more.

• The theater must operate under a LORT-Equity contract, which varies according to the size and budget of the theater.

In addition members must individually subscribe to and be bound by LORT's bylaws and any collective bargaining agreements between LORT and any union representing employees of the applicant. There is no question that each LORT theater is not-for-profit and clearly professional. The seventy-seven members represent some of the United States's largest and most prestigious companies. A brief examination of a few member theaters, large and small, will further describe the kind of organization LORT is.

The Alley Theatre is a LORT company in Houston, founded in the late 1940s by Nina Vance. By the 1950s the Ford Foundation proclaimed the Alley "the most significant professional theater outside of New York." The Alley staged the premiere performances of Paul Zindel's *The Effect of Gamma Rays on Man-in-the-Moon Marigolds,* Frank Wildhorn's musical version of *Jekyll & Hyde,* and Paula Vogel's *The Baltimore Waltz,* among other works. Budget in 2006 was $11 million.

The Long Wharf Theatre was founded in New Haven, Connecticut, by two Yale alumni, Jon Jory and Harlan Kleiman, in 1965, when Arthur Miller's *The Crucible* opened for a two-week engagement. Michael Christofer's *The Shadow Box* premiered at Long Wharf and earned its author a Pulitzer, and D. L. Coburn was

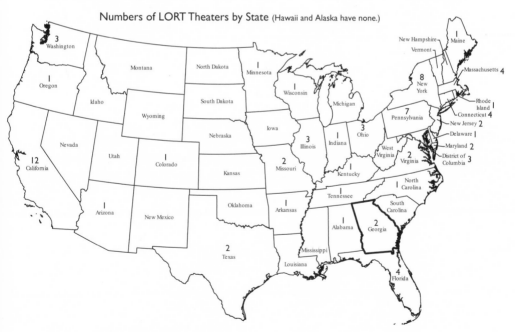

Fig. 6.1 LORT theaters are concentrated on the west and east coasts of the U.S., as is the population.

awarded the Pulitzer Prize after his *The Gin Game* transferred from Long Wharf to Broadway. The Long Wharf, a LORT theater, has a $6.5 million budget and an audience of more than one hundred thousand each year.

Since 1985, the mission of the **Shakespeare Theatre Company** in Washington, D.C., has been to present classic theater in an accessible, skillful, imaginative, American style that honors the playwrights' language and intentions while viewing their plays through a twenty-first-century lens. Growing out of the Folger Library, the Shakespeare Theatre Company moved into a new theater, the Harman Center for the Arts in 2007. The center has two acting spaces, the 774-seat Sidney Harman Hall and the 451-seat Lansburgh Theatre. The Shakespeare Theatre Company's revenue in 2007 exceeded $9 million.

LORT theaters include some less well known nationally than these three, including Florida's Maltz Jupiter Theatre and the Marrimack Repertory Theatre in the Boston area. **The Marrimack Repertory Theatre** draws more than forty thousand audience members yearly to its productions which include new plays and challenging contemporary scripts. Its budget is about $2.4 million. **The Maltz Jupiter Theatre** grew out of a dinner theater founded by Burt Reynolds in the late 1970s and became a not-for-profit theater in 2004. On a budget in excess of $4 million, the Maltz Jupiter presents a season of crowd-pleasing musicals and comedies.

The Alliance of Resident Theatres / New York

Founded in 1972 by 49 off-off-Broadway companies, including Manhattan Theatre Club, Playwrights Horizon, Classic Stage Company, and Repertorio Español, this trade group was first known as the Off Off Broadway Alliance (OOBA). Today it is made up of 266 professional not-for-profit theaters in New York City and is known as the Alliance of Resident Theatres / New York (A.R.T./NY).

Full membership requires a theater be an incorporated 501(c)3 not-for-profit theater that has produced two full seasons in New York City. Further a member must be a professional theatrical producing organization with performances open to the general public. A.R.T./NY does not define *professional* in its membership requirements. It's clear, however, that the two top tiers of members—defined as having budgets from $1 million to $5 million and in excess of $5 million—are leaders in the universe of New York City's not-for-profit professional theaters.

Thirty-four Largest A.R.T. / NY Theaters by Budget

Tier 1A ($5 million and up)
Lincoln Center Theatre
Roundabout Theatre

Tier 1B ($1 million–$5 million)
3–Legged Dog

The Acting Company
Atlantic Theatre Company
Classic Stage Company
Collaborative Arts Project 21
Dance New Amsterdam
Dance Theatre Workshop
ENACT
HERE Arts Center
Irish Repertory Theatre
La MaMa e.t.c.
Labyrinth Theatre Company
Mabou Mines
MCC Theatre
Folksbiene National Yiddish Theatre
The New Group
New York Musical Theatre Festival
New York Theatre Workshop
Pearl Theatre Company
Playwrights Horizons
Pregones Theatre
Primary Stages
Queens Theatre in the Park
Second Stage Theatre
Signature Theatre Company
SITI Company
Summer Play Festival
TADA!
Vineyard Theatre
Wingspan Arts
Women's Project & Productions
York Theatre Company

League of Chicago Theaters

Founded in 1979, the League of Chicago Theatres (LCT) describes itself as a trade and marketing association for its more than 175 members. Not all LCT members are not-for-profit, or even theater organizations. For example, the full membership list includes the Chicago Symphony, Chicago Gay Men's Chorus, several college/university theaters (including Northwestern University), Cerqua Rivera Dance Theatre, and Light Opera Works. Professional commercial theaters are also league members.

In fact members range from storefront, nonunion theaters with yearly budgets under ten thousand dollars to major cultural centers with multimillion dollar productions. LCT was first launched to manage a discount ticket booth in downtown Chicago called Hot Tix. Perhaps the opportunity to sell tickets through Hot Tix encouraged so many diverse arts organizations to join the LCT. The league now offers a full range of services aimed at strengthening theater operations in an increasingly challenging cultural and economic environment. Its membership is truly diverse.

The history of the LCT has been replayed in other cities with substantial performing arts communities. One example is the LA Stage Alliance, primarily a marketing group supporting a community of more than 325 professional, educational, community-based producing and performing arts organizations in the Los Angeles area.

The LCT should not be confused with the Chicago Area Theatre (CAT) Equity Contracts. This Equity agreement is used by theaters with a capacity of nine hundred seats or fewer within thirty-five miles of the Chicago city limits. In 2008 the Chicago office of Equity estimates that there were forty-one CAT contracts, all of them issued to not-for-profit theaters. Those CAT contractors include some of the largest and best known of the Chicago theater community: Goodman Theatre, Steppenwolf Theatre Company, Chicago Shakespeare Theatre, and Lookingglass Theatre Company.

Seasonal Outdoor Theater

The Institute of Outdoor Drama, founded in 1963, is the trade organization for more than one hundred constituent theater companies. All members are not-for-profit theaters. Thirty-seven produce historical dramas, nine stage religious dramas, five primarily offer musicals, and fifty-six are Shakespeare festivals. The institute estimates these companies hire approximately five thousand people each summer. Its membership includes such stalwart companies as Paul Green's *The Lost Colony* (founded in 1937) and *Unto These Hills* (founded in 1950), both in North Carolina as well as *Tecumseh!* (founded in 1970) in Ohio, and *The Great Passion Play* (1968) in Arkansas. Musical theaters include the Jenny Wiley Theatre (founded in 1965) in Kentucky. Several seasonal Shakespeare festivals are members, including the Tony Award–winning Utah Shakespearian Festival (1962) and the Oregon Shakespeare Festival (1935).

The Institute of Outdoor Drama gathers information related to the writing, management, and production of outdoor theater. It distributes this information to production companies, the news media, and artists in the field. Although several of these outdoor theaters are affiliated with Actors Equity Association and are professional in all meanings of the word, the institute makes no claim that its members are professional.

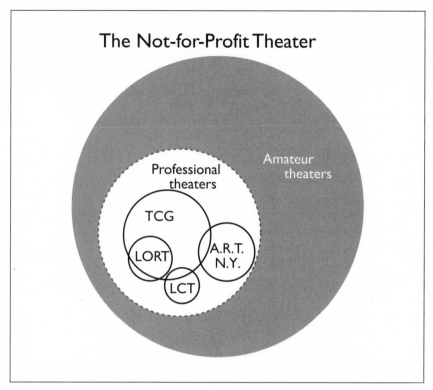

The Not-for-Profit Theater

Professional theaters

Amateur theaters

TCG

LORT

A.R.T. N.Y.

LCT

Fig. 6.2 Professional theater is a subset within not-for-profit theater. Within that subset, no single organization embraces all professional not-for-profit theaters. To further complicate the picture, LCT and A.R.T./NY have members which are commercial theaters or not theaters at all. That complexity is not shown in the Venn diagram above.

Diversity No Single Organization Defines

There is surprisingly little overlap among these many organizations supporting largely or solely not-for-profit theaters (see fig. 6.2). Only 24 of A.R.T./NY's 266 members are members of TCG. All but 18 of LORT's 77 members are members of TCG. Only 15 of the more than 175 members of LCT belong to TCG. Fourteen of the Institute of Outdoor Drama's 107 members belong to TCG. Thus there is no single association to define and represent the professional not-for-profit theater in the United States.

If there were definitive criteria for being a professional not-for-profit theater, certainly some theaters would find them unsatisfactory. Recall the Economic Census definition of a professional actor noted earlier, in which only someone who earned the bulk of his or her income from acting in the week prior to the survey was a professional actor. This definition can be applied rigorously, which is good, but it cuts the number of self-defined professional actors in the United States at least by one-half, probably by more.

The problem of separating professional from amateur theaters is not a problem for the not-for-profit theater community, only for those who study and parse the community's makeup. Instead of being a problem, it is one expression of theater's protean quality. The diversity of not-for-profit theater shows the drive and ambition of those who form, support, work for, and grow these regional theaters. What theaters survive and grow depends on many factors, artistic, managerial, and financial.

Financial Profile of Not-for-Profit Professional Theaters

Although TCG's membership is not synonymous with the country's not-for-profit professional theater universe, TCG has been surveying its members on financial matters since at least 1999. Members of TCG identify themselves with the professional not-for-profit theater and pay what can be significant member dues, 0.175 percent of the theater's total income with a minimum assessment of $500 and a maximum assessment of $10,000. A theater with a $200,000 budget would be assessed $500. A $1 million theater would be assessed $1,750. The eighteen TCG theaters with budgets over $10 million pay the maximum assessment of $10,000 per year. TCG's survey figures, collected at considerable expense, are the best available and are a valuable resource for those interested in theater management and finance in the United States.

Not-for-profit professional theaters, judging from TCG's member surveys, vary greatly in size. More than one-third have budgets of less than $500,000. Extrapolating from TCG's reported budgets gives an estimate that the smallest one-third of TCG theaters account for about 3 percent of the budgets of all the TCG theaters combined. The 19 largest theaters in TCG have combined yearly budgets of more than one-third of a billion dollars, accounting for an estimated 37 percent of the budgets of all TCG not-for-profit theaters combined. The list of these largest theaters includes many of the best-known names in the not-for-profit professional theater universe.

Theater	Budget
McCarter Theatre Center	$10,500,000
The Children's Theatre Company	$11,500,000
North Shore Music Theatre	$12,000,000
Steppenwolf Theatre	$12,347,284*
Denver Center Theatre Company	$12,400,000
Chicago Shakespeare	$13,000,000
La Jolla Playhouse	$13,500,000

Arena Stage	$14,440,518*
Alley Theatre	$14,741,000
Goodman Theatre	$14,925,000
Public Theatre	$17,375,466*
American Conservatory Theatre	$19,000,000
Guthrie Theatre	$19,500,000
Shakespeare Theatre Company	$19,600,000
The Old Globe	$20,500,000
Oregon Shakespeare Festival	$23,500,000
Roundabout Theatre Company	$30,000,000
Lincoln Center–Vivian Beaumont	$47,052,455*

These budget dollar figures are the approximate budgets for 2006–7 as listed in the TCG online database. Those marked with an asterisk did not list a budget in TCG's records so the budget is taken from the most recent IRS Form 990 available. A few TCG members are part of larger institutions with work other than theater and are not included, such as the Kennedy Center for the Performing Arts in Washington, D.C.

Missions and Histories of Not-for-Profits Are Highly Varied

Not-for-profit theaters have a great range of interests and missions. The following profiles are chosen at random.

Kitchen Dog Theater, Dallas, Texas—Budget about $250,000

"It is the mission of Kitchen Dog Theater to provide a place where questions of justice, morality, and human freedom can be explored. We choose plays that challenge our moral and social consciences and invite our audiences to be provoked, challenged, and amazed."

Borderlands Theater, Tucson, Arizona—Budget about $210,000

"Borderlands Theater is a professional theater company recognized nationally and internationally for . . . programs that reflect the diversity of the voices of the Southwest border region . . . focusing on the Latino/Chicano/Mexicano voice as the core voice to nurture and support. . . . The 'border,' both as physical and social landscape, is a metaphor for Borderlands' work."

Diversionary Theatre, San Diego, California—Budget about $500,000

"Diversionary Theatre was founded in 1986 to provide quality theater for the lesbian, gay, bisexual, and transgender communities. The mission of the theater is to produce plays with gay, lesbian, and bisexual themes that portray characters in their complexity and diversity both historically and contemporarily."

The Ensemble Theatre, Houston, Texas—Budget about $1.5 Million

"The mission of The Ensemble Theatre is to preserve African-American artistic expression; to enlighten, entertain, and enrich a diverse community."

Missions and Histories

Generally people start not-for-profit theaters because they feel a need for artistic expression for themselves, their communities, or some underrepresented minority group. The stories of how three not-for-profit theaters grew to prominence in the last half century are telling. These brief synopses give a sense of the way not-for-profit theaters start and grow.

Perseverance Theatre

Determined to start a theater, when Molly Smith graduated from American University in Washington, D.C., she dragged fifty old theater seats back home to Juneau, Alaska, a land-locked community of thirty thousand souls. In 1979 she borrowed ten thousand dollars from her grandmother and looked around for talent. Smith said, ""If I needed an actor, I'd go into a bar and pull somebody off of a bar stool and say, 'Do ya' wanna be in a play?'" She interviewed thirty-five oldtimers, casting six of the best storytellers for her first production, *Pure Gold*. "They were people who'd come up with the gold rush or it was Filipinos who were working in the mines or of course it was the Native Americans, the Tlingit people, who've been there for centuries. And the audiences were hungry for it. They were hungry for it because it was part of what had drawn people to Alaska. So this theater company was very much about really plumbing the resources of what there was in Alaska." Now Perseverance Theatre has a yearly budget just more than $1 million and is respected in its community and around the nation.

Steppenwolf Theatre Company

In 1974 two high school seniors and a recent graduate of Highland Park High School got together to produce *And Miss Reardon Drinks a Little*. They borrowed a church in nearby Deerfield, Illinois, and called their company the Steppenwolf Theatre Company. One of the three was reading the Herman Hesse novel *Steppenwolf* at that time. Three more plays were produced under this first incarnation of Steppenwolf. One of these, *Rosencrantz & Guildenstern Are Dead,* reunited high school pals Terry Kinney, Jeff Perry, and Gary Sinise. During this production the friends decided that, when they were finished with college, they would find a permanent space and would attempt to start a professional resident ensemble theater company. In the years since, Steppenwolf Theatre Company in Chicago has received national and international recognition from media, theater critics, and audiences alike. They now have assets in excess of $30 million, revenues greater than $13 million a year, and twenty thousand subscribers.

Roundabout Theatre

Gene Feist and his wife, actress Elizabeth Owens, conceived Roundabout Theatre Company in 1965. Feist, who wanted to do classic plays, thought that a subscription series at an affordable price would interest New Yorkers. Roundabout's
first production, Strindberg's *The Father,* was presented in a 150-seat theater in
the basement of a supermarket in Chelsea. In that first season, the company had
400 subscribers who paid five dollars for three plays. Although the growth of
Roundabout was not a straight line—they went into bankruptcy in 1978—this
not-for-profit is now a major force in American theater. The Roundabout operates three Broadway theaters, the American Airlines Theatre, the Henry Miller
Theater, and Studio 54, and the off-Broadway Laura Pels Theatre as well as a 99-
seat studio theater. They have 40,000 subscribers and a budget in excess of $30
million.

Next: Incorporation

A not-for-profit theater starts with an artistic idea, but very soon, if it is successful and survives, it must incorporate so that it can solicit financial support. Becoming a corporation also protects the principals from being personally liable for
the debts of the theater. As long as no one does anything illegal, the only assets that
are at risk for an incorporated theater, as stated previously, are those of the corporation. Nonprofit corporations can take advantage of other benefits, such as special postage rates and, in many communities, property tax exemptions.

A corporation also may survive the loss of any given participant in the corporation. For example, Molly Smith founded Perseverance Theatre and after nineteen years left it to head the Arena Stage in Washington, D.C. Perseverance continued and grew to new successes first under the direction of Peter DuBois (now
the associate producer at New York's Public Theater), then P. J. Paparelli (formerly associate director of the Shakespeare Theatre in Washington, D.C.), and
Art Rotch, a fourteen-year-veteran Perseverance designer and member of IATSE
Local 829.

A corporation must choose a name that complies with the state's corporation
rules and file formal "articles of incorporation" together with a filing fee. There are
skeleton models of appropriate articles of incorporation that simplify the process.
The first board of directors must be appointed and meet, create corporate bylaws,
and define the operating rules for the corporation. The initial board of directors
will elect subsequent board members, according to the bylaws. It is the board of
directors that actually runs the corporation for the benefit of the community identified in the not-for-profit mission statement. It is this defining fact—that the not-
for-profit theater is run by a board of directors that is self-perpetuating—that lets
the corporation survive the loss of a principal member. In practice not-for-profit
organizations differ in the extent to which the board of directors is active in the

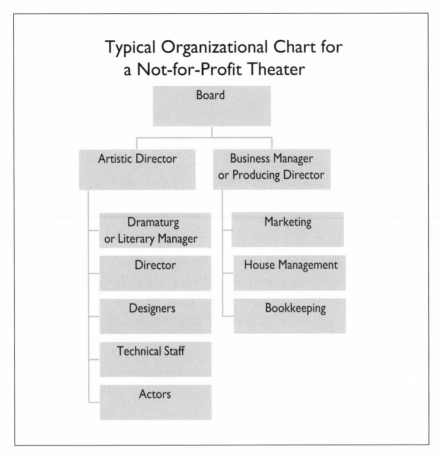

Fig. 6.3 A typical organizational chart for a not-for-profit theater. In practice, for many not-for-profit theaters, the board is a rubber stamp for the artistic director's initiatives.

management of the theater. In early years boards may be little more than a necessity to meet legal requirements. But healthy and long-lived organizations have boards that are independent of, albeit cooperative with, the artistic and financial management of the theater (see fig. 6.3). To that end bylaws and theater operating procedures in long-lived organizations draw lines about what board members are allowed to control and how they exercise that control.

Real-life Board Involvement

Every three years TCG surveys its member not-for-profit theaters about their boards and practices. In 2004 the survey found the average size of theater boards was twenty-six individuals. Of these, 85 percent made personal contributions to their theater's annual fund. In many theaters the board's greatest duty is to raise funds for the theater either from its own pockets, the companies board members work for, or friends recruited to contribute. On average, according to TCG, 12 percent of operating funds and 39 percent of capital campaign funds of surveyed theaters come from board members. In fact a high percentage of theaters, 77 percent, *require* board members to contribute financially to the theater, often with suggested or required minimum amounts. Board members commonly have high annual individual incomes, averaging $140,630. Theaters with larger budgets tend to have board members with higher annual incomes than do small theaters.

Most theaters have written descriptions of board responsibilities. The trend over time has been for greater professionalization of not-for-profit theater boards, with increased board development procedures such as orientations, retreats, and self-assessments. The TCG report concludes, "Governing board members are charged with the important task of strengthening theaters' artistry and fiscal stability simultaneously. A successful board enhances a theater's public standing in its community and ensures that the theater has adequate resources to fulfill its mission." Board members in the survey tend to believe the key measure of a theater's success is financial stability, the least important measure is the quality of reviews. In this the board reflects its essential function, the continuance of the organization through time. More than half of the boards also have formal evaluation procedures for their artistic and business directors.

Not-for-Profit Theater Income and Expenses

The following data comes from the 2006 TCG survey of member theaters. The survey is used here not to make definitive statements about the not-for-profit professional theater universe in the United States, but rather to get a general idea of where the money for the not-for-profit professional theater comes from and where it goes to.

Earned Income

On average about 62 percent of the budget for surveyed not-for-profit theaters is earned income. Tickets account for about 44 percent of budget. The rest of earned income comes from a number of small sources such as endowment earnings, capital gains, concessions, and rental. The percentage varies depending on the size of the theater, with the smallest group (with budgets less than five hundred thousand dollars) getting 38 percent of budget from earned income to the largest group (with budgets greater than $10 million) making 70 percent from earned income. Large established theaters are more efficient at funding themselves from ticket sales than small theaters (see fig. 6.4).

Subscription tickets made up less than half of ticket sales. Subscription sales have trended downward since 2001. Advance ticket sales have been diminishing

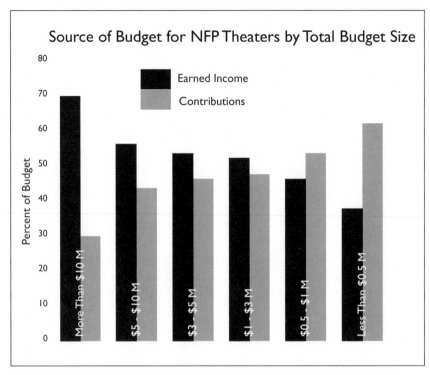

Fig. 6.4 Larger theaters get a larger portion of their budgets from box office.
Source: 2006 TCG Survey.

as well, both for commercial and not-for-profit theaters. Average not-for-profit
ticket price was $27.38, with prices varying with budget size. The average ticket
price for theaters with the largest budgets was $39.84; the smallest theaters had an
average ticket price of $17.43. Theaters sold an average of 71 percent of available
seats. Here, too, the outcomes varied with budget size. The largest theaters by
budget sold 80 percent of capacity; the smallest sold 59 percent.

Contributed Income

Contributed income is, of course, the obverse of the earned income figures. Contributions range from 77 percent of budget for the smallest theaters to 41 percent
for the largest. Contributions from trustees and other individuals were the largest source of nonearned funds, averaging 17.5 percent of budgets (see fig. 6.5).
Foundations gave 9.3 percent of budget on average, with corporations accountable for another 5.1 percent. Government provided an average of 6.3 percent, with
about half of that coming from state government. The federal government provides only 0.7 percent of not-for-profit professional theater budgets on average.

The remaining small amounts come from in-kind donations, united arts funds, and "other contributions."

Income More Than Total Budget in 2006

The figures for earned and contributed income added up to more than 100 percent in 2006. This is a result of the average theater having a surplus. Total income from earnings and contributions was typically almost 109 percent of budget.

Expenses

Payroll makes up about 54 percent of budget for not-for-profit theaters (see fig. 6.6). When a not-for-profit theater is in financial straits, payroll is inevitably the first thing cut. Fund-raising costs are notably small, at 3.6 percent. Not-for-profit theater's fund-raising costs as reported are well in line with those of other charitable organizations. A survey of the largest charitable organizations in the

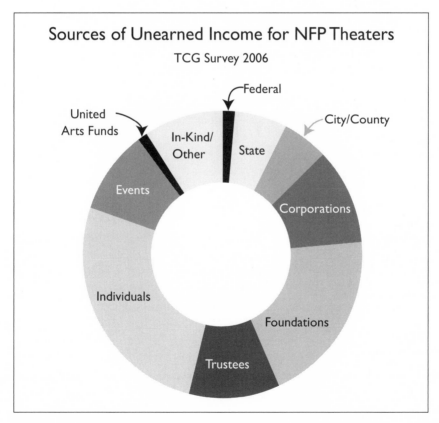

Fig. 6.5 The largest source of unearned income for NFP professional theaters is individual contributions.

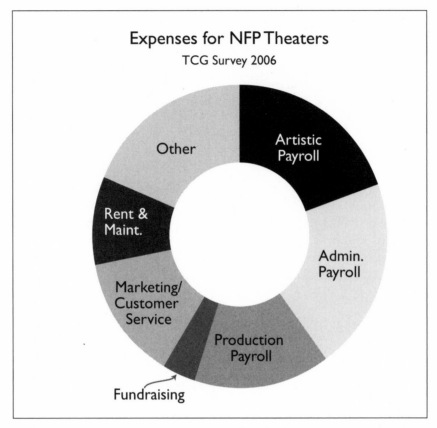

Expenses for NFP Theaters
TCG Survey 2006

Other · *Artistic Payroll* · *Rent & Maint.* · *Admin. Payroll* · *Marketing/ Customer Service* · *Production Payroll* · *Fundraising*

Fig. 6.6 Payroll dominates expenses for the NFP professional theater.

United States, using IRS 990 reports as the source of the data, showed average fund-raising costs of 4.6 percent. However, the IRS data rarely include all the costs of staff, board, and volunteer time devoted to fund-raising, according to the Association of Fundraising Professionals (AFP). When the value of the hours spent on fund-raising by staff that is not totally devoted to fund-raising is included, the cost for the AFP-surveyed organizations was 18 percent of budget. We imagine that the not-for-profit theater's reporting of fund-raising costs is similarly understated.

Top Not-for-Profit Theater Leaders' Salaries

The chiefs of the biggest not-for-profit theaters make big salaries. Some question if the salaries are commensurate with the duties. Andre Bishop, artistic director of the Lincoln Center Theatre, who was paid more than four hundred thousand dollars in the 2007 season, said, "I receive a handsome salary and worked 35 years to get it. . . . The idea that because we're nonprofit we shouldn't earn a decent living is ludicrous. We're the CEOs of a company with a budget of about $35 million." The other head of the Lincoln Center Theatre, Executive Producer Bernard Gersten, also receives more than four hundred thousand dollars per year.

The Lincoln Center CEOs are not unique. Roundabout Theatre paid Artistic Director Todd Haimes more than $475,000 in 2007; the board recently awarded him with an additional $3.2 million if he stays until May 7, 2018. The award is intended to buy an annuity to provide retirement benefits to Haimes. Lynne Meadow and Barry Grove for the Manhattan Theatre Club received more than $476,000 each that year. The Public Theater paid its artistic director, Oskar Eustis, a little more than $275,000. By comparison the general manager of the Metropolitan Opera, Peter Gelb, was paid just over $1 million in his first year in that position.

The Minneapolis–St. Paul newspaper, the *Star Tribune,* reported in January 2009 that the area arts community was "buzzing" about the disclosure that Joe Dowling, director of the Guthrie Theater, was paid $682,229 in salary and benefits in 2007. A Guthrie board member was quoted as saying, "It's a lot of dough, especially in this economy, but I don't think his pay is excessive. The Guthrie is the largest regional theater in the country, with three stages going. . . . He's done a heck of a job, both fiscally and artistically." The Guthrie Theater, named after its founder Sir Tyrone Guthrie, opened in 1963. The IRS filing for 2006 places its budget at more than $32 million.

Although individual contributors may blanch at these salaries, folks knowledgeable in philanthropic management are not concerned. James Steinberg, a director of the Harold and Mimi Steinberg Charitable Trust, noted, "It's a lot of money but they all bring in a lot of money and relative to the CEOs of for-profit corporations, it's nothing." The median salary of chief executives of 249 nonprofits that provided data to a recent survey of the *Chronicle of Philanthropy* was $326,500.

Life Cycle of Not-for-Profit Professional Theaters

By many financial measures, large not-for-profit theaters are better off than small theaters. (But the *importance* of a theater is not judged by its size. Since this book is about the finances of the professional theater, we leave the evaluation of artistic and community impact to others.) It's tempting to imagine that the greater financial health of larger not-for-profit theaters reflects a life cycle to not-for-profit theaters.

The Four Stages of the Business Life Cycle

Business schools teach that all businesses experience four stages in their life cycles: startup, growth, maturity, and decline/transfer. There is no set time of each stage. The needs and stresses of each stage of development differ. The life cycle of organizations leads to a pyramid structure of existing businesses at any one time, with many in startup, fewer who have managed the challenges to survive into the growth stage, fewer still in the mature stage, and only some of these making the transition into transfer/decline.

Start-up

In the early days the hours are long. The new business has few or no employees, maybe working out of the founder's home. The business needs capital, but, without a cash flow record, loans are hard to come by. This is a high-risk period, when the business's viability is unclear. Many start-ups fail at this stage.

Growth

When the growth stage is in full swing, sales increase, and it's hard to keep up. Staff is increasing. Time and energy are spent to find talented people and keep them. The necessary financing to support growth is difficult too, but, with some record of growth, more banks will consider loans and investors can be found. Funding the growth—in inventory, receivables, physical plant—is the crucial risk in this period. Without cash management even profitable businesses in the growth stage can go under or fall into technical bankruptcy, with the owners losing control of the business. Thus growth is stressful and leads many businesses in this phase of the life cycle to fail.

Maturity

In maturity the business has survived the growing pains and is making a profit. There is increased prestige in the industry and community. The value of the business assets is substantial. The length of the maturity phase is unpredictable.

Decline/Transfer

The fourth stage of the business life cycle is often called *decline,* but it doesn't have to be that. The business may still be going strong. Often the original founders are reaching the age and wherewithal to consider retirement, philanthropy, or other activities. It's time to transfer the reins of power if that hasn't been done already, bringing in new vigorous leadership. The new owners may continue to run the business as it has been in the past, or they may wish to explore other options and go through the life cycle again.

Similarity of Not-for-Profit Theater Life Cycles

How does this relate to not-for-profit theaters? Fairly directly, in our experience. Even nonprofessional community theaters often go through these cycles. The professional not-for-profit theater certainly does, and each stage can be a crisis for the inexperienced leader or leaders.

As theaters grow, the skills that are needed change, and the growth is wrenching for the original happy band of theater artists who first said, "Let's put on a show!" In a start-up, the artistic director may also be the managing director and sometimes the usher and janitor. If the organization is to grow, specialization must enter into the picture, and some person or people must take on the obligation to recruit, hire, train, and, if necessary, fire staff, even if the staff members are volunteers. Not every artistic personality is prepared to take on these new duties.

Imagine that many of the smallest theaters in the TCG study are in the start-up or growth phase. Some will grow, and some will die. The failure to thrive may come from a lack of skills needed to manage the organization and attract contributors. Or theaters may fail because the mission of the founders does not match up with a sufficient audience in the community. Of course, some small theaters are fully satisfied with their productions and impact at the size they are and do not wish to grow.

Averages Hide Important Differences

As valuable as the TCG surveys are, they hide a wealth of difference among the not-for-profit theaters in the United States. Some theaters are professional versions of community theaters, whose seasons comprise unchallenging classics, musicals, and comedies that middle-class Americans are said to favor.

Another subgroup of not-for-profit theaters specializes in programming with a regional appeal. For example, the American Folklore Theatre, playing on an outdoor stage at Peninsula State Park in Wisconsin, specializes in developing new musicals with regional themes. Its shows have included the adventures of John Muir, father of America's national parks, and the music of James Taylor. Its musical about ice fishing, *Guys on Ice,* has been produced in other regional theaters.

Other not-for-profit professional theaters specialize in specific audiences or subjects. Theater Rhinoceros in San Francisco "develops and produces works of theater that enlighten, enrich, and explore both the ordinary and extraordinary aspects of our queer community." It has done so since 1987. There are also not-for-profit professional theaters that focus on classic plays. The Pearl Theatre Company, New York City, gets respect and positive reviews for a "repertory strongly rooted in the classics [that] offers to the company, and demands of the company, scope, resonance, and variety. . . . It is essential to the health of the theater and to the craft and souls of theater artists to keep vital our rich tradition." In Chicago, since 1974, Victory Gardens Theater has been "dedicated by mission to serving playwrights and producing world premiere plays." Victory Gardens Theater received the 2001 Tony Award for Best Regional Theater.

Intermission

Steppenwolf Theatre Company and
the Stages of Financial Growth

Located in Chicago, Steppenwolf Theatre Company calls itself an "international performing arts institution committed to ensemble collaboration and artistic risk through its work with its permanent ensemble, guest artists, partner institutions, and the community." The history of Steppenwolf is a concrete example that a not-for-profit professional theater must survive financial growing pains that accompany success.

Financial Stability Today

Steppenwolf is a major force in the U.S. theater, developing new plays and inculcating a strong physical acting and directing style in its ensemble members. Steppenwolf's IRS 990 report for 2005 reveals total income of $13.2 million, expenses of $12.3 million, with a surplus for the year of just under $900,000. It knows how to raise money. Most of the unearned income was from direct support, which was in excess of $4.7 million. Government support was just over $100,000; government support for the average not-for-profit theater is minor. Steppenwolf spent $1.1 million on a gala fund-raising event that netted them just over one-half million after expenses. They had earned income from a parking structure and rental of spaces, touring, earnings on the endowment, and so on, of $1.7 million. The rest, about $6 million, came from ticket sales.

Steppenwolf has had surpluses for each of the last five years; so, at the end of 2005, its cash reserves totaled just over $23 million. Such cash reserves are essential for weathering the unexpected losses that might arise from a string of unpopular productions or some world event that would negatively affect ticket sales or fund-raising.

The largest item in expenses is salaries and benefits totaling a little over $6 million. Supplies cost more than a half million. Printing is nearly a half million, and advertising is over $700,000. Steppenwolf's sources of income and types of expenditures, by percentage, are comparable to the average large theater surveyed by TCG, theaters with budgets over $10 million.

Income Source	Steppenwolf	TCG Large Average
Direct support	35%	30%
Government support	<1%	6%
Ticket Sales	43%	48%
Interest	<0.5%	1%
Fund-raising events	4%	5%
Other Rev	16%	10%

Expenses	Steppenwolf	TCG Large Average
Salaries and Benefits	50%	54%
Administration	39%	30%
Depreciation	6%	3%
Supplies	5%	13%

Steppenwolf expenses come from the IRS 990 form and the average expenses for large not-for-profit theaters from the 2006 TCG survey. The two sources do not use the same terms so the authors indulged in some informed guesses in generating percentages for comparison.

As described previously, the stages of the business life cycle are start-up, growth, maturity, and decline/transfer. These stages are an intellectual construct, a guide to understand and even predict a growing organization's needs. No entity passes clearly through each stage. Steppenwolf, for example, has cycled repeatedly through growth and maturity.

In 2003 the Nonprofit Finance Fund (NFF) published a fascinating study of the financial impact of the growth of Steppenwolf Theatre. NFF is a provider of financial resources, in the form of loans, grants, and asset-building programs, in concert with management advice to nonprofit organizations. Much of what follows is informed by the NFF account, but the application of the business life-cycle model to Steppenwolf's history is ours.

Stage One: Start-up

Steppenwolf, founded by Kinney, Perry, and Sinise in 1974, incorporated in 1975, and reorganized in 1976 to expand membership, was initially housed in an 88-seat facility located in the basement of the Immaculate Conception Church and School in Highland Park, Illinois, which rented for twenty-five dollars a month. In a few years the troupe moved into a converted garage, with 211 seats and a rent of more than thirteen hundred dollars a month.

According to the NFF study, the board of Steppenwolf did hardly any governing in the first few years. The board supplemented the theater's box office take with a little money and loaned kitchen chairs for the audience to sit on to keep the theater going. This is typical for new not-for-profit organizations of all stripes; their start-up stage is driven by a founder or small group of founders.

In these early years, Steppenwolf's financial assets consisted of a little equipment and a little cash from the box office. In 1982 the actors wanted to mount Brecht/Weill's *The Threepenny Opera*. The board recognized that even if the show sold out the two hundred seats, there wasn't enough money to support the production as envisioned, so they vetoed the production. This was the first time the board asserted itself. "It was a cold shower for both the board and the ensemble— an early step in the gradual, sometimes painful transformation of an artistic phenomenon into a cultural institution of international stature. . . . Sinise recalls, 'we started to look at ourselves as more of a company and not just a bunch of kids in a basement doing plays.'" Earned income in calendar year 1982—mostly from ticket sales—approached $200,000, contributed income raised by board members was about $20,000, and grants totaled $79,000. But even without staging *The Threepenny Opera*, the year ended with Steppenwolf in the red by $13,000.

Stage Two: Growth

As a result of the deficit, the board was expanded and drew in more of "Chicago's downtown leadership." The new board members were not as wealthy as those of Chicago's more established not-for-profit institutions, but there were more professionals, corporate executives, and foundation officials.

Moving from 88 to 211 seats made sense since Steppenwolf was selling out most performances. But a bigger theater's costs—in rent, increased production values, and promotion—outpaced earned income and made the failure of any given show threaten the theater's continued existence. In this period the box office produced 75 to 80 percent of the theater's income, and some costs were artificially low because of the sweat equity from the artists, their families, fans, and volunteers.

This is a financial conflict that arises in the early growth stages of new organizations, commercial *and* not-for-profit: how to get cash to fund growth and how to professionalize what had theretofore been an informal organization. Growth is good but dangerous. Steppenwolf still faced the possibility that one or more unpopular shows could produce crippling losses or chase away the unpaid work force. What was at stake financially was still low if Steppenwolf had failed at this time. Steppenwolf had no real estate, no investors, and few employees.

The financial challenges, however, didn't reduce the artistic quality of the productions. Steppenwolf had striking artistic success during this period of its growth. We still vividly remember a night in October 1982—early in this period of Steppenwolf's life cycle—taking a New York subway on a rainy night downtown

---

No Business Life Cycle in the Commercial Theater

Not-for-profit theaters that succeed go through a life cycle because they are corporations that continue, in theory, eternally. The commercial theater produces a single play for a given partnership/company and then disbands. Commercial productions must succeed by opening night. After opening, there is no time for growth or improvement. A producer in the commercial theater may learn and grow through time, but a commercial production does not have a life cycle.

---

to the Cherry Lane Theatre to see a show that had gotten good reviews. The production was Steppenwolf's staging of Sam Shepard's *True West*, the first show Steppenwolf brought to New York. At intermission we scrambled through the program, asking, "Who are these two incredible actors?" They were John Malkovich and Gary Sinise, Steppenwolf company members whose names would be noteworthy again and again for stage, film, and television work over the next quarter century. Mel Gussow writing for the *New York Times* called the Steppenwolf transfer "an exhilarating confluence of writing, acting, and staging. . . . *True West* is acted for its reality even when the events are surreal."

Stage Three: Maturity

The new theater and the structural changes made in the board helped to consolidate Steppenwolf into its mature stage of the organizational life cycle. A product of this stage again wowed audiences outside of Chicago.

By 1990 Steppenwolf had taken to Broadway, London, and California its original staging of John Steinbeck's novel *The Grapes of Wrath*. The *New York Times'* Frank Rich wrote that this production was "pure theater as executed by a company and director that could not be more temperamentally suited to their task. . . . [Steppenwolf] is an ensemble that believes in what Steinbeck does: the power of brawny, visceral art, the importance of community, the existence of an indigenous American spirit that resides in inarticulate ordinary people."

At the end of this period, many of the early company members were going on to success elsewhere. Joan Allen was becoming well-known in film, and Sinise was directing film. Glenne Headley had eight movies to her credit and was nominated for an Emmy for *Lonesome Dove*. Malkovich made his first two films in 1984—*Places in the Heart* and *The Killing Fields*—and completed his eighth in 1988, *Dangerous Liaisons*. He spent his time in Chicago, New York, London, Hollywood, and the south of France.

A Vital Organization Grows Again

Even with some comfort in its mature stage, the company was ambitious and looked to shore up its standing. The board was radically transformed again, based on a study the theater commissioned in 1987. Steppenwolf recognized that it had become a community asset, and the community saw its governance as a community trust. The study determined that the board needed more senior professionals and top-ranked executives. The board grew to twenty-nine members and would continue growing, reaching forty-two members in five years. Board members had to meet explicit quotas for money contributed or raised, and time spent volunteering, as well as attending regular meetings.

The year after *The Grapes of Wrath,* Steppenwolf's accumulated cash and investments were $4.6 million; this money came from the surpluses of several years, not from a capital fund-raising effort. Money in the bank is insurance for an ambitious not-for-profit theater, a resource to see it over a period when experiments don't pan out with critics, audiences, and donors. But, for most every show, Steppenwolf was selling out and had a waiting list for returned tickets.

The next step seemed clear: a new, bigger theater. Current artistic director Martha Lavey said, "This is a group of very ambitious people. They are not going to be limited to one theater or even one city. So our theater has to be good enough, including big enough, to keep their loyalty." The new theater was estimated to cost $9 million. The building would be valued at three times the group's previous annual revenue. One board member said that up to that point, "We had never raised a penny of capital [for an endowment or a building]. We were a $3 or $4 million, basically breakeven operation." Building a new theater promised to stretch the organization just to raise the money.

They had great success and luck, both in the fund-raising and in the construction. The building came in on time and on budget. The resulting building includes two theaters, the Downstairs Theatre with 515 seats and the Upstairs Theatre with 299 seats. In 1996 Steppenwolf bought an adjoining parking garage, providing a new source of income and, on the ground floor, a new theater, the Garage Theatre, a black box seating about 100, with tickets costing twelve dollars.

A new building with two or three times the seating doesn't mean just doubling or tripling the ticket revenue. "It means paying—in perpetuity—for hard assets that must be constantly made to generate revenue. In effect, a company whose main product had been art is now also formally in the business of managing real estate—hungry seats and square feet that depreciate, need repairs, insist on being heated and cooled and cleaned, whether they are empty or full," as the NFF report put it. Steppenwolf became not just a bigger theater but also a developer, landowner, and debtor. This observation is not hyperbole. In getting bigger, Steppenwolf also became a fundamentally different organization. Thus they entered a new period of change and risk to the company's future existence.

Fixed costs need to be paid with predictable revenue—more predictable than ticket sales—meaning in this case an endowment and contributions from a larger and more diverse set of supporters. To manage the new responsibilities, the number of regular employees grew from forty-six in 1994 to eighty-two in 1996. The development department grew from three people to thirteen in the same time. Unearned income covered 50 percent of budget by the end of the 1990s. With a renewed emphasis on subscribers, seasons were determined in advance so they could be sold as seasons. No more "to be announced" on the schedule.

With this increased activity in hiring, organizing, and fund-raising, the board's workload increased as well. The full board meets less often now than it did before, but committees meet frequently. The executive committee of the board meets monthly, and the finance committee meets six to eight times a year. In 2008 the theater had an endowment over $10 million—more life insurance for an artistically vital, risk-taking organization.

Stage Four: Transfer—Not Decline

As happens with all successful organizations if they grow, the company has become something the early ensemble had never imagined. Good thing, too, as the original founders are entering the next stage in their lives; Steppenwolf must be passed to others to maintain, grow, and change. Martha Lavey wrote, "Plenty of companies die because the founders can't imagine replacing themselves. The Steppenwolf founders and those original members of the company took another tack: They dared to believe that what they had created had real endurance and they sought to sustain and grow that dream. . . . It is, finally, our job to replace ourselves. We commit to the transfer of what we know to younger artists who will, in their own turn, teach us something new."

New facilities and wealth have led to new areas of artistic activity: a new plays lab, a nontheater series called "Traffic," an incubator for younger Chicago theater groups, and the School at Steppenwolf. Steppenwolf productions have moved to other regional theaters. In 2006 *Red Light Winter,* written and directed by Adam Rapp, played the Barrow Street Theatre in New York; *Love-Lies-Bleeding,* directed by Amy Morton and featuring ensemble member Martha Lavey, was presented at the Kennedy Center in Washington, D.C.; *The Bluest Eye,* directed by Hallie Gordon, went to the New Victory in New York; and *The Sunset Limited,* featuring ensemble member Austin Pendleton, played at the 59E59 Theaters in New York.

In December 2007 Steppenwolf again stormed Broadway. They had commissioned a play from company member Tracy Letts; the result was *August: Osage County.* The original Steppenwolf cast, with the exception of the underage child in the company, opened at Broadway's Imperial Theatre. In the *New York Times,* Charles Isherwood declared *August* to be "flat-out, no asterisks and without qualifications, the most exciting new American play Broadway has seen in years." The

Steppenwolf company of actors was lauded for "the harsh humor, ferocity, and keen feeling of their performances." In December 2008, the Steppenwolf cast of *August: Osage County* opened at the National Theatre, London, while the Broadway production continued its run.

At roughly the same time that *August* opened in New York, Steppenwolf founding member Laurie Metcalf was appearing in a commercial Broadway production of a new political satire by David Mamet, *November.* She told the *New York Times,* "It's so great to have 'August: Osage County' playing one block away. . . . The fact that we're all here, we had the holidays together, go to parties together —I get to see more of the Steppenwolf crowd here in New York than I have for many years in Chicago." Steppenwolf has always had a loose ensemble that was free to pursue other opportunities. Metcalf's history is a good example; she is probably best known for playing Roseanne Barr's sister on the hit television comedy series *Roseanne,* which ran eleven years.

Steppenwolf is now a mature and vital organization that is continually transferring its mission to a younger generation of artists and managers. A strong core of feeling, a sustained artistic philosophy, and what must be a very savvy and flexible board of directors has kept Steppenwolf growing and healthy through the years and the life cycle of not-for-profit theater companies.

7

●●

Shall We Dance?

*The Commercial and Professional
Not-for-Profit Theater Relationship*

Today the fates and fortunes of many not-for-profit theaters are intertwined with those of the commercial theater in ways that were unimaginable thirty years ago. It's a dance, and like dance it requires communication, grace, trust, and art.

The entrepreneurial spirit of the not-for-profits began only after the first Broadway transfer of the not-for-profit production *The Great White Hope* enhanced the reputation of the regional theater that originated it but provided it no revenues. In contrast the potential financial reward of a successful Broadway transfer was demonstrated eight years later when the Public Theatre developed *A Chorus Line.* That legendary musical helped support the Public, a not-for-profit theater, for fifteen years; it was for a time the longest-running Broadway musical in history.

The contrast between the financial outcomes of these two productions are touchstones of the history of not-for-profit theaters in the United States that are devoted to the development of new plays and musicals. The productions were successes in every measure, but one redounded financially to the originating not-for-profit theater, and one did not. Once the art is taken care of, it's all about the money.

Arena Stage, 1967

The Great White Hope, a new play by Howard Sackler, opened in 1967 at not-for-profit Arena Stage, Washington, D.C., supported in part by grants from the National Endowment for the Arts. The original cast, which included James Earl Jones and Jane Alexander, moved to a commercial production on Broadway in 1968. This was the first time a regional theater production with its cast appeared on Broadway. The play ran for 546 performances on Broadway and was later made into an esteemed film.

The Great White Hope is a fictionalized biography of African American boxing champion Jack Johnson, named in the play Jack Jefferson. Placed in the early decades of the twentieth century, the story had strong topical allusions for 1960s audiences, for the play expresses how segregation and prejudice defeated Johnson/Jefferson. The play won the Pulitzer Prize and three Tony Awards. This was James Earl Jones's first big role; he received the Tony, and he was nominated for a best acting Oscar for the film. The play was also a breakthrough in the career of Jane Alexander, who received a Tony for her performance on Broadway and was also nominated for an Oscar.

Arena Stage received no royalties or other payment as the play it fostered went on to success on Broadway and in film. Arena didn't even get a credit in the Broadway *Playbill*. The original production was budgeted by Arena Stage at a fifty thousand–dollar deficit, which the not-for-profit theater took on because of the importance of the subject matter and themes. Of course, within the community of people who closely followed theater in the United States, Arena Stage did get an enormous boost in prestige and respect. Indeed the transfer of *The Great White Hope* engendered a new respect for the whole category of not-for-profit professional theaters across the United States.

The Public Theatre, 1975

A Chorus Line opened off-Broadway at the not-for-profit Public Theatre on May 21, 1975. It is set on a bare stage at an audition of dancers for a Broadway musical. The musical was unconventional for its time for not having a plot; instead dancers assembled at an audition tell snippets of their biographies and sing about their aspirations. The entire limited run sold out immediately. Just two months later, on July 25, it opened on Broadway at the Shubert Theatre, where it ran for 6,137 performances, grossing $64 million on Broadway alone. It won the Pulitzer Prize and nine Tony Awards. It held the distinction for a time of being the longest running show in Broadway history.

A Chorus Line was produced on Broadway by Joseph Papp, artistic director of the Public Theatre, and much of its earnings redounded to the Public. Estimates of the earnings to the Public from *A Chorus Line* vary, from $10 million to $20 million. The earnings, whatever their total, freed the Public from many financial worries for fifteen years.

The Nexus of the Not-For-Profit and Commercial Theatres Today

Between these two totem productions is where the not-for-profit theater finds itself today. Not-for-profit professional theaters that originate new material are demanding a financial reward should the plays or musicals become commercial successes. Other not-for-profit theaters are entering into cooperative arrangements with commercial producers to stage first or early productions of new work with financial support from the producers in the form of *enhancement money*. And in New York City a small number of highly influential not-for-profit theaters are filling in some of the artistic space left by the commercial theater's general neglect of new nonmusical plays, important revivals, and challenging new musicals. Of course, it's just a small percentage of America's not-for-profit professional theaters that are dancing with the commercial theater. In truth most regional theaters are just that: wed tightly to their respective regions or communities.

As noted earlier, about one-quarter of Broadway shows since the 1999–2000 season have been produced by not-for-profit theaters on Broadway and 60 percent of the "Best of . . ." Tony Awards given since 1999–2000 have been for shows produced by or originated in the not-for-profit theater. In total 55 percent of Broadway productions had their origins in the not-for-profit theater from 1999–2000 to 2007–8. An additional 14 percent during this period were imported from other countries, usually Great Britain. And since 1976 the Pulitzer Prize for drama has been awarded almost solely to plays originated in the not-for-profit theater. The lone exception is Neil Simon's *Lost in Yonkers*.

Part of the reason for the not-for-profit theaters' importance in new play development is that a significant number of founders and leaders of the not-for-profit theater put an emphasis on new play development and on creating relationships with emerging playwrights. This is the heroic work of the U.S. theater: high-risk research and development for our cultural capital. Unlike new work in nonperforming arts, a new play can only be appreciated and developed with actors, designers, directors, and, most of all, audiences. The not-for-profit theaters that devote some or all of their energies to new play development are doing the heavy lifting for our theater.

The other reason for the not-for-profit theaters' importance in new play development is that the commercial producers have mostly left the field, preferring to cherry-pick the best of the not-for-profit and London arenas, or choosing to use the not-for-profit theaters when developing new material. It's all about money. Broadway producers develop little new work for a number of financial reasons.

First, most new plays do not succeed. We have already noted how risky new play production is and why. Let us just add one cheeky comparison: baseball. Babe Ruth's career home run count of 714 stood as the record for thirty-nine years. His batting average was great at .342. But that batting average means that two-thirds of the time he went to the plate, the result was an out. About new product development, the CEO of world consumer product powerhouse Proctor & Gamble referred to the baseball player Pete Rose in describing his approach to innovation: "You get up more times, you get to swing the bat a few more times, you get a few more hits. . . . In the innovation game, which is a risky game, more 'at bats' leads to more 'hits.'" Even the best in their field fail and fail repeatedly. By harvesting already successful material, the producers believe the odds are improved.

Second, taking a show for an out-of-town trial, leading to an opening on Broadway, is very expensive. The creative folks behind the musical *The Producers* estimated that the out-of-town run in Chicago increased the show's budget by $2 million. Even a sold-out out-of-town tryout does not necessarily pay for itself. For a comedy show, *The Producers'* producers thought a trial run was essential. New shows need to be experienced in front of audiences to be developed and improved—and judged. It's an expensive process. The minimal investment to open a work on Broadway is large, typically for a straight play a minimum of $2 million and at least $10 million for a musical. That expenditure is reduced when a producer uses enhancement money to see a show on its feet, in front of an audience in a not-for-profit regional theater. How enhancement money works is discussed later in this chapter.

Commercial producers will go to great lengths to reduce the cost of mounting a new show. In 2009 John F. Breglio first staged his revival tour of the musical *Dreamgirls* in South Korea. His South Korea partner Shin Chun Soo covered many costs, including the $1.5 million for the sets. The Korean performers did not come with the sets; the show was recast.

Third, reading a pile of unsolicited scripts is significant work. Someone must be paid to do the work. By cherry-picking the best of the regional and foreign theater, a commercial producer relies upon those other theaters to make the first sifting through all the possible new material.

Finally, not-for-profit theaters enjoy union concessions that reduce costs at many levels. For example, if a commercial producer stages a workshop of a new production, Equity requires that the actors and stage manager involved share 1 percent of gross revenues from most future commercial productions of the material. However, if the workshop is produced through a not-for-profit entity, Equity doesn't define it as a *workshop*. No matter: the function for the producer is the same, and, in the case of the not-for-profit trial staging or workshop, the performers get no such financial entitlement.

The 2008 musical *Cry-Baby* was first produced by the not-for-profit La Jolla Playhouse in California with enhancement money from the intended Broadway commercial producers. A rehearsed staged reading of the script and songs was held in New York for 150 invited guests, with a cast of 25, organized under the auspices of the La Jolla Playhouse. The cost of the workshop was $276,760. The performers received $728 per week for their work, a little more than the Equity workshop minimum of $606 a week. But the performers acquired no share in future revenues, a substantial savings had *Cry-Baby* been a Broadway success. It wasn't; it flopped.

And—more about marketing than finance—Broadway producers have appreciated working outside of the media spotlight in New York and the traditional nearby tryout cities of Boston, Philadelphia, and Washington. However, the Internet now has undermined the isolation of regional theaters, especially for development of new productions with famous names attached.

Despite the interdependence between the not-for-profit and commercial theaters—or maybe *because* of the interdependence—the relationship between them is emotionally complex. Arvin Sponberg, in his book *Broadway Talks,* describes the relationship: "Condescension, resentment, envy, and distrust exist to be sure. The idea of tax-exempt subsidy is especially galling to people who pride themselves on paying their own way. But the commercial theater's leaders are shrewd enough to realize that their own future is irrevocably linked to the health of the not-for-profit theater."

Successful collaborations breed additional collaborations among the parties. The U.S. theater industry is small enough that word of bad faith spreads quickly. And the creative process requires trust. Remembering the experience of Arena Stage, the not-for-profit theater knows it must not only trust the commercial producer but also write a good, clear contract.

Financial Involvement of Not-for-Profits in New Plays

Not-for-profit theaters entering into agreements with playwrights to develop and/or produce new scripts generally require, by contract, both billing in future incarnations of the material *and* ongoing financial participation. A typical agreement might call for the not-for-profit to receive 1 percent of gross receipts and 5 percent of net profits from any commercial productions. More established not-for-profit theaters might require 2 percent of gross and 10 percent of profit. Typically this financial participation by the originating theater expires after a time, often around three years. The theory is that if the play is not picked up for commercial production quickly, the not-for-profit theater's original production did little to enhance the script's value. For example, Playwrights Horizons asks for 10 percent of the playwright's proceeds from subsidiary rights. The Roundabout Theatre requires 40 percent. Lincoln Center Theatre takes no share in subsidiary rights.

The difficulty in negotiating these agreements is that a playwright may be anxious to see a full staging of a new script and ready to agree. But if the playwright agrees to very high future financial involvement of the originating not-for-profit, commercial producers may later find it hard to craft a production with enough profit potential to attract investors.

It is increasingly common for the not-for-profit to acquire an exclusive right to produce a commercial transfer of the play, either alone or with coproducers. This gives the not-for-profit a dominant say in the commercial future of the material as well as the hope of greater financial return should the play be a commercial hit. In addition, originating not-for-profit theaters will frequently require a share of the author's income from future not-for-profit productions of the material, *if no commercial production is forthcoming,* typically 5 to 10 percent of the author's income after agent commissions.

Smaller, economically challenged not-for-profit theaters may be satisfied with billing as the originating producer of a script without financial remuneration. Such a theater sees a connection with a successful new play as a major marketing opportunity, enhancing the theater's status within its community and increasing donor support. As an attorney specializing in entertainment law slyly remarked, this unwillingness to pursue all financial streams potentially available to these small theaters "may explain [why] some are struggling to meet payroll on a weekly basis."

The Feeders

The term *feeder* is used informally to refer to the not-for-profit theaters that repeatedly produce work that is later found stage worthy on Broadway. Outside of New York, theaters that have earned the sobriquet of feeder include the Intiman (Seattle), Seattle Repertory Theatre, Old Globe Theatre (San Diego), Center Theatre Group (Los Angeles), South Coast Repertory (Costa Mesa, California), Steppenwolf and the Goodman (Chicago), Long Wharf Theatre (New Haven, Connecticut), and a newcomer, Geffen Playhouse (Los Angeles), among others. In New York, feeders include the Second Stage Theatre, the Atlantic Theatre Company, the Public, and a few others.

It must be emphasized that the history of readings, partially staged productions, workshops, and the like can be complex and hard to trace for any new play. Picking out these feeder not-for-profits for particular discussion doesn't begin to tell the whole story of the development of new plays. And the development of new scripts doesn't have to lead to Broadway to be successful. The repeated production of a script in the leading not-for-profit regional theaters in the United States and maybe in London is a very rich outcome for the playwright and, if not as great a financial return, at least a potent psychological payback. Such an outcome also provides the playwright an enhanced knowledge of playwriting craft and of collaboration with producing entities. Additionally, repeated mountings build name recognition, useful when the playwright's next play is ready for its first staging.

Consideration of a modestly budgeted theater in the Midwest and a large theater on the West Coast provides a quick overview of *feeders.* These kinds of not-for-profit professional theaters outside of New York City are focused on producing new plays.

Lookingglass Theatre

Lookingglass Theatre has gained a sort of fame for two things: a founding member is David Schwimmer, who went on to star in the hit television comedy series

Friends, and Lookingglass was chosen to be the resident theater company in the historic Water Tower Power Plant in the Magnificent Mile area when the City of Chicago remodeled it in 2003. Prior to occupying the Water Tower, Lookingglass was an itinerate theater, performing in different rented or borrowed spaces. Lookingglass, formed in 1988 by a group of recent college graduates who sought to develop new plays, has produced forty-five world premieres and has received forty-two Jefferson Awards and citations. The Jefferson Award is a respected Chicago-area recognition of theater excellence.

Lookingglass developed *Metamorphoses,* a staging of some tales of Ovid, written and directed by company member Mary Zimmerman. The production was a success in Chicago, with the run extended seven times by popular demand. Then Second Stage, a New York City not-for-profit, presented the production in its 2002 season. The play went on to a commercial run of four hundred performances at the Broadway theater Circle in the Square. *Metamorphoses* grossed nearly $10.5 million on Broadway.

In the 2006–7 season, Lookingglass staged three new plays that transferred to or were produced by other theaters. Mary Zimmerman's *Argonautika* has been staged since the Lookingglass premiere production at the Berkeley Repertory, the Shakespeare Theatre (Washington, D.C.), and the McCarter Theatre (Princeton, N.J.). Also that season, it produced the first play by J. Nicole Brooks, *Black Diamond.* The play was nominated for a Jefferson Award and later received a staged reading by the Classical Theatre of Harlem. The company's adaptation *Lookingglass Alice* that same season was presented at the Arden Theatre Company (Philadelphia), the New Victory Theatre (New York), and the McCarter.

Lookingglass is clearly one of the not-for-profit theaters developing important new work. It produced five shows in the 2005–6 season on a budget of about $2.3 million; about half of that was for salaries and wages. Lookingglass also spent just over $500,000 on its education and outreach programs, bringing its total budget to $2.8 million. Ticket sales were just over $675,000, or under 30 percent of program expenditures. Net assets were about $4 million.

Seattle Repertory Theatre

The founding story of the Seattle Rep is unusual for it starts with a building, not an artistic group or individual. In 1962 Seattle's successful World's Fair left behind the Seattle Playhouse. In the following year, Seattle Repertory Theater was founded, largely through the efforts of real-estate magnate Bagley Wright, one of the original investors in Seattle's Space Needle and, with his wife Virginia, a major art collector and patron of the arts. The first artistic director was the peripatetic Stuart Vaughan. The theater came of age in the 1980s under Daniel Sullivan as artistic director. Since 2005 Sullivan has remained involved as artistic consultant.

The Seattle Rep has three performance spaces: 856 seats, 286 seats, and 99 seats. It's a member of the League of Resident Theatres (LORT) and so is a union house, engaging Equity actors, SDC directors, and IATSE stagehands. Staff totals about 300; it plays about 300 performances a year.

According to its own description, the Seattle Repertory Theatre is "committed to producing the world's finest dramatic works, engaging our audiences in a shared exploration of the most pressing issues of our time . . . , arts education programs, and a series of new play development programs." In forty-four years, it has developed ninety-four new plays through its New Play Workshop and Hot Type New Works festival. Twelve shows that originated or workshopped at Seattle Rep have gone on to Broadway runs.

In its 2005–6 season, Seattle Rep produced a new adaptation by Shelley Berc and Andrei Belgrader of Carlo Gozzi's *The King Stag,* Ariel Dorfman's *Purgatorio,* and Amy Freed's *Restoration Comedy,* which had been developed with Seattle Rep and other not-for-profit theaters. Its Women Playwrights Festival staged four new works. Together with the Kennedy Center in Washington, it imported *Cathay: Three Tales of China* from the Shaanxi Folk Art Theater in China. It rounded out the season by presenting to the Seattle theatergoing population several recent plays developed or premiered elsewhere, including August Wilson's *Golf Radio,* Heather Raffo's *9 Parts of Desire,* and Jeffrey Hatcher and Mitch Albom's *Tuesdays with Morrie.*

The 2008 IRS 990 filing shows the Seattle Repertory Theatre had a yearly budget of $10.4 million. More than $5.7 million of the budget, about 61 percent, went to personnel. A little more than 40 percent of the budget came from the box office; most of the rest came from direct public support. The theater reported $6.2 million in assets, less than one year's budget. But the Seattle Repertory Theatre Foundation, whose purpose is to support the Rep, holds assets worth more than $17 million, made up of highly liquid investments plus some government securities.

Second Stage Theatre

Second Stage Theatre is one of two New York City not-for-profit theaters specializing in new play development. These demonstrate that even with low-to-moderate budgets, not-for-profit theaters can be successful feeders of the commercial stage. Director Carole Rothman and actress Robyn Goodman founded Second Stage Theatre in 1979 to give "second stagings" to contemporary American plays that originally failed to find an audience. From there Second Stage has evolved to developing new plays as well. Since 1988 Second Stage has originated six shows that transferred to Broadway. In the 2005–6 season, Second Stage produced six plays, all but one a new script. Its new play development program presented eight readings of plays and two musical workshops.

The budget for Second Stage Theatre, based on the 2008 IRS filing, was more than $7.6 million. Personnel costs were about $3.6 million, or about 45 percent of budget. Box office and subscriptions totaled a little more than $3 million, about 50 percent of budget. Second Stage received $227,043 in royalties in 2006, presumably as payment for its role as one of the producers of the Broadway run of *The 25th Annual Putnam County Spelling Bee,* which it originated off-Broadway. Second Stage will join the other not-for-profit theaters presenting on Broadway when it buys and operates the Helen Hayes Theatre.

The Vineyard Theatre

The Vineyard Theatre is dedicated to new plays and musicals. Since 2003 two Vineyard Theatre productions have transferred to Broadway, *Avenue Q* and *[title of show].* Through the 2007–8 season, Vineyard has staged two or three productions a year. The 2005–6 season counted *[title of show]; Stopping Traffic,* a one-woman show by Mary Pat Gleason; and *Miracle Brothers,* a new musical by Kirsten Childs. In the 2007–8 season, Vineyard staged three new plays, *The Piano Teacher* by Julia Cho, *The Slug Bearers of Kayrol Island, or, The Friends of Dr. Rushower* by Ben Katchor and Mark Mulcahy, and *God's Ear* by Jenny Schwartz.

The Vineyard manages this on a budget in 2005–6 of $2.2 million, of which about half is for payroll. Box office income is only $320,783, less than 15 percent of budget. But the Vineyard got more than five hundred thousand dollars in royalties, presumably from the Broadway run of *Avenue Q.*

Enhancement Money

With the financial advantages of the not-for-profit professional theater noted earlier, it was inevitable that commercial producers should become actively involved with not-for-profit professional theaters. The primary mechanism for that involvement today is *enhancement money.*

Enhancement money is a donation given by a commercial producer to augment the budget for a show at a not-for-profit theater. Enhancement money is given in cases where the commercial producer already has options for the work in question. It is a *donation* because the commercial producer has little say in the not-for-profit production's development. The producer is looking mostly for knowledge about the script's readiness for commercial exploitation. The regional theater, in addition to getting a substantial increase in the average budget for a show, shares to some extent in any future profits of the show. If the material to be produced is a match for the regional theater's mission, its audience has the opportunity to experience new material and to share psychically in the excitement of future commercial productions, if any occur. The commercial producer generally has a right to purchase the physical assets of the production, such as sets and costumes, but doesn't always do so.

A sophisticated production of a new musical at a big not-for-profit theater might cost more than a million dollars. Should the not-for-profit typically budget five hundred thousand dollars for revivals of musical shows, it cannot afford the new musical as part of its schedule. But an interested producer may pony up enhancement money of the remaining amount to see the not-for-profit staging. For almost any venture, five hundred thousand dollars is a major investment, but not so major when contrasted with the money needed to stage a major musical on Broadway, at least $10 million and often much more. With enhancement money contributed to a not-for-profit theater, the potential commercial producer learns much about the material's viability with audiences for a relatively low cost. In addition a successful regional production makes it easier for the producer to attract investors for a Broadway run.

In New York City enhancement money supported not-for-profit Manhattan Theatre Club's musical *The Wild Party* and a nonmusical play, *Current Events,* in 2000. Neither transferred to Broadway. Also in the year 2000, the Jewish Repertory Theatre had enhancement money for Arthur Laurent's play *Big Potato:* no transfer to a commercial run. The New Group's revival of *What the Butler Saw* got enhancement cash but no transfer. Primary Stages received enhancement money for three 2000 productions and not one went commercial. Enhancement money supported *Modern Orthodox* at New Haven's Long Wharf Theatre that year. No luck. This litany of failure to make a commercial transfer doesn't show that enhancement money is a jinx. Rather it confirms that new productions are risky. Producers who put up enhancement money for these productions saved themselves the bigger losses they would have incurred if they'd gone directly to a much more expensive commercial run that flopped. In recent years a couple of not-for-profit theaters seem to have specialized in enhancement deals for large new musicals.

La Jolla Playhouse

Since 1984 the La Jolla Playhouse, located on the University of California San Diego campus, has been involved in 16 shows to transfer to Broadway, including nine musicals. Musical successes have included *The Who's Tommy, Big River,* a revival of *How to Succeed in Business without Really Trying,* and *Jersey Boys.* Not all the musicals La Jolla originated went on to Broadway success; consider *Jane Eyre* (ran for twenty-five weeks on Broadway), *Cry-Baby* (eight-week run), and *Dracula, the Musical* (twenty-week run). La Jolla has also developed straight plays and concerts that went on to Broadway, including *A Walk in the Woods, 700 Sundays, The Farnsworth Invention,* and *I Am My Own Wife.*

La Jolla Playhouse, according to its publicity materials, "advances theater as an art form and as a vital social, moral, and political platform by providing unfettered creative opportunities for the leading artists of today and tomorrow."

Founded in 1947 by movie actors Gregory Peck, Dorothy McGuire, and Mel Ferrer, La Jolla Playhouse became inactive in the 1960s but was revived in 1983. Des McAnuff served as artistic director from 1983 to 1994, returning as A.D. again from 2000 to 2007. The theater is currently led by Artistic Director Designate Christopher Ashley, Managing Director Steven B. Libman, Associate Artistic Director Shirley Fishman, and "Director Emeritus" Des McAnuff.

Big River, a musical based *The Adventures of Huckleberry Finn,* ran on Broadway for more than one thousand performances beginning in 1985. It grossed $19 million for this run and has become a favorite of regional and amateur theaters in the years since. La Jolla produced *Big River* with sixty-five thousand dollars in enhancement money from Dodgers Productions, the eventual lead producer on Broadway. In addition La Jolla received 1.5 percent of box office grosses and 3.75 percent of net profits from the commercial run.

Jersey Boys, a musical built around the life and tunes of Frankie Valli and the Four Seasons, opened on Broadway in 2004 and was still running as 2009 begins. It has grossed more than $243 million on Broadway. Checking *Variety* listings in May 2008, the Broadway *Jersey Boys* was at 100 percent of capacity in its fourth year, grossing more than $1 million a week in New York alone. The show had two national tours and a successful Las Vegas company. La Jolla's original production received $900,000 in enhancement money from Dodgers Productions. La Jolla gets 1 percent of gross receipts, going up to 1.25 percent at recoupment, in addition to 3 percent of profits.

Des McAnuff directed these musicals. In 2007 McAnuff, born and raised in Toronto, became an artistic director for the Stratford Shakespeare Festival in Canada, a $60 million Canadian not-for-profit theater. McAnuff produced the action-adventure film *Iron Man,* which opened to strong box office in 2008 as well. He is now working as film director and screenwriter on a "monster musical project" to be produced by Disney Productions.

All these shows were produced, at least in part, by Dodger Theatricals and usually played in Jujamcyn-owned theaters. And Des McAnuff was one of the founders of Dodger Theatricals in the mid-1970s. Another cofounder was Rocco Landesman, who was first the director of Jujamcyn Theatres and co-owns the company. Landesman was made NEA chair in 2009.

Dodger Theatricals earned a solid reputation on Broadway in the 1980s with critically acclaimed productions, including *Big River, Into the Woods,* and *The Gospel at Colonus.* In the 1990s Dodger suffered financial setbacks, but it has been buoyed in the new millennium by providing production services to other producers and, of course, *Jersey Boys.*

La Jolla Playhouse runs on a budget of about $12.3 million, according to the IRS 990 filing from 2005. This was a substantial leap over the previous year's budget of around $8 million. The increase is probably a result of the opening in 2005 of a third performance space at La Jolla, the Sheila and Hughes Potiker Theatre. About one-half of the budget is for personnel. La Jolla earned just over one-quarter million in royalties and $1.2 million from coproductions for this year.

In addition to providing La Jolla with income, the commercial productions that originated there provide royalties to their director, Des McAnuff. In 2005, McAnuff's salary from La Jolla Playhouse was $100,000. In addition, La Jolla paid almost $250,000 to Skunk, Inc., a New York City corporation of which Des McAnuff is director. The purpose of this payment according to the IRS 990 form is "theatrical production." In the not-for-profit theater's 2002 IRS 990, the purpose of a $189,690 payment to Skunk, Inc., was listed as "artistic director." Skunk, Inc., appears to be a privately held corporation; no further information about it could be found. One imagines this payment is additional compensation to McAnuff. Some tax experts advise theater professionals with variable yearly income to create corporations to receive some or all of their salaries, thus to even out the tax effects of good and bad years.

The Old Globe

Another not-for-profit theater with significant experience with enhancement money, the Old Globe, is also located in San Diego. Since 1987 the Old Globe has originated nine musicals that transferred to Broadway, as well as seven nonmusical plays.

The Old Globe Theatre was built in 1935 for the presentation of abridged versions of Shakespeare's plays as part of the California Pacific International Exposition. At the conclusion of the exposition in 1937, a not-for-profit group leased the theater from the city. In January 1981 the theater's board of directors established the Globe as a year-round professional company with Jack O'Brien as artistic director. O'Brien has directed most of the commercial transfers and has in recent years worked separately from the Globe, directing opera, developing musicals in other producing organizations, and directing for New York City's not-for-profit Lincoln Center Theatre, most notably the first New York productions of the plays of Tom Stoppard. The Globe produces fifteen mainstage productions yearly, ranging from Shakespeare to an ongoing emphasis on the development and production of new works. It performs in three theaters, the Old Globe Theatre seating 580, the outdoor Lowell Davies Festival Theatre seating 615, and the 250-seat Sheryl and Harvey White Theatre.

The Old Globe budget for 2005–6 was a little over $17 million. About 55 percent goes to personnel. More than 58 percent of revenues come from ticket sales. During the last three years for which IRS reports are available, the Old Globe has received significant amounts of enhancement money: $1.5 million (2006), $1.4 million (2005), and $3.3 million (2004). In 2006 Old Globe premiered the Broadway-bound Bob Dylan musical *The Times They Are A' Changing;* in 2005, the

Broadway-bound *Chita Rivera: The Dancer's Life;* and, in 2004, the Broadway-bound *Dirty Rotten Scoundrels:* two flops and a hit, respectively. As a result of the successful shows the Old Globe originated, it received royalties each year, including more than $114,000 in 2006.

Enhancement money and the royalties from a show that transfers to a commercial run can be important sources of revenue to a not-for-profit theater, just as the successful Broadway transfer is a source of pride to the regional theater and the community it serves. Even established and financially secure regional theaters such as La Jolla and the Old Globe understand the importance of pursuing all sources of funds that do not conflict with their charitable missions. It also doesn't hurt if the opportunities and royalties that successful transfers offer their talented and ambitious artistic directors keep those directors motivated and attached to their respective not-for-profit organizations.

Super-NFPs

Remember that three not-for-profit theaters produce on Broadway: the Lincoln Center Theatre, the Manhattan Theatre Club, and Roundabout Theatre. They are sometimes called the *super-nfps.* By producing on Broadway, these organizations and the artists whose work appears on their Broadway stages are eligible for Tony Awards. Perhaps because of this, these organizations are able to attract name-brand performers who might not, except for this fact, appear in the not-for-profit theater. The big three theaters also operate smaller off-Broadway venues and still smaller studio theaters.

These three groups also have an entrepreneurial spirit. When the Lincoln Center Theatre has a hit show in its Broadway house, the Vivian Beaumont Theatre—"hit" meaning in this case a show with demand greater than the usual limited run can fulfill—it is willing to turn the production into an open run and move later shows on its season to a rented Broadway house. Lincoln Center did so when the dance musical *Contact* ran at the Beaumont in 2000–2002, grossing more than $60 million. *Contact* received the Tony Award for Best Musical, Best Featured Actor and Actress in a Musical, and Best Choreography. *Contact's* Drama Desk Awards included Outstanding New Musical, Outstanding Featured Actress in a Musical, Outstanding Choreography, and Outstanding Lighting Design. Lincoln Center is pursuing the same strategy during the run of the rapturously received 2008 revival of *South Pacific.* LCT's artistic director André Bishop said, "Because it's the same contract [for performing by a not-for-profit in a commercial Broadway house], it's the same expense for us. . . . Also, this allows me to pick plays that I can't normally do. Proscenium plays like *Awake and Sing* or *The Heiress* or *The Delicate Balance* would not have worked well in [the Beaumont's] thrust space." Similarly the Roundabout played its 1998 revival of *Cabaret* at the Studio 54 as an open run. *Cabaret* played 2,377 performances, grossing more than $119 million dollars.

The super-nfps also bring into New York City productions from London and elsewhere for which commercial producers cannot be found. The Roundabout *Cabaret* was brought in from a successful production at London's not-for-profit Donmar Warehouse. In the 2007–8 season, Roundabout imported from London a camp new play based on the Hitchcock movie of *The 39 Steps* and transferred the production to a commercial run after its not-for-profit limited run. Also in that season it brought in from London a high-tech revival of *Sunday in the Park with George.* This production originated at the Menier Chocolate Factory Theatre, a 190-seat London fringe theater. *The 39 Steps* originated at North Country Theatre in Richmond, North Yorkshire, played London's Tricycle Theatre, and went on to a commercial run in London's Criterion Theatre.

Importing significant London productions for limited Broadway runs was once the province of old-time commercial producers of the second half of the twentieth century, such as Alexander Cohen and David Merrick. Today London transfers are another instance of super-nfps filling roles in the Broadway theater that the commercial theater has neglected.

Manhattan Theatre Club

One of the super-nfps began as an off-off-Broadway showcase producer in 1970. Manhattan Theatre Club is "solely dedicated to producing new plays and musicals." It has a subscriber base of twenty thousand and produces seven plays a year in Broadway's recently restored Biltmore Theatre on West 47th Street, now named the Samuel J. Friedman Theatre, and at its off-Broadway venues in the City Center complex. MTC transfers plays to commercial runs on a semiregular basis. Three examples of transfers include Charles Busch's comedy *The Tale of the Allergist's Wife,* David Auburn's drama *Proof,* and John Patrick Shanley's drama *Doubt,* which became a successful movie.

According to MTC's 2006–7 annual report, the company's artistic development staff evaluated more than one thousand scripts that season, held twenty-eight play readings and four musical readings, and commissioned new scripts under a grant from the Alfred P. Sloan Initiative. MTC offers seven rehearsed public new play readings each season, a program called "7 @ 7."

MTC's budget for 2007 was more than $22 million; about one-half of that went to personnel. More than $10 million of revenue came from ticket sales. Nearly $3 million came from royalties from the commercial runs of shows originated at MTC. Net assets totalled $32 million, about one-and-one-half times its yearly budget. MTC owns at least one for-profit corporation, MTC Productions, Inc., which serves as the lead producer for commercial transfers and tours of productions originated by the not-for-profit entity.

The Roundabout

The Roundabout Theatre's troubled early history, including a spell in bankruptcy, was mentioned earlier. After two years with Todd Haimes at the artistic helm, beginning in 1983, the Roundabout emerged from bankruptcy. It later moved to a Broadway house and now operates three Broadway houses, the American Airlines Theatre, the Henry Miller Theatre, and Studio 54, along with an off-Broadway theater and a studio space. The mission of the Roundabout when it began was to revive classic plays and musicals. In 1995 it started to develop and produce new works. It has forty thousand subscribers.

In the 2006–7 season, Roundabout held thirty-three play readings and workshops and presented eight full productions. Roundabout produced for the first time a touring production; its revival of *Twelve Angry Men* played nineteen cities for 256 performances and continued touring in 2007–8. For its first year the tour was financially successful, accounting for 13 percent of Roundabout's costs but 18 percent of Roundabout's income. Excluding the tour, Roundabout productions in 2006–7 played to nearly five hundred thousand audience members, at 87 percent of theater capacity.

All these productions, plus some New York City educational activities, were performed with a budget of $47.5 million, of which a healthy 72 percent came from ticket sales. Royalties from new plays developed at Roundabout amounted to about $162,000. As with most not-for-profit theaters, about half of the budget went to personnel.

Roundabout is inventive in seeking out all revenue streams, even controversial ones. Some theater professionals turned up their noses when Roundabout licensed the name of its premier Broadway theater on 42nd street, formerly known as the Selwyn Theatre, to American Airlines for a reported $850,000 a year for ten years: $8.5 million total.

Most not-for-profit theaters are the sole producers of their seasons, and for years this was true for the Roundabout. Increasingly Roundabout playbills list associate producers. In 2002 Roundabout was one of the associate producers of a stellar revival of Arthur Miller's *The Crucible,* starring Liam Neeson and Laura Linney, which played at the Virginia Theatre, owned by Jujamcyn. The producing credits were amazingly long:

> Produced by David Richenthal, Manocherian / Leve / Boyett, Max Cooper, Allan S. Gordon, Roy Furman, Us Productions, Élan V. McAllister, Adam Epstein and Margo Lion; Produced in association with Dede Harris, Morton Swinsky, Clear Channel Entertainment, Old Ivy Productions, Jujamcyn Theaters (James H. Binger: Chairman; Rocco Landesman: President; Paul Libin: Producing Director; Jack Viertel: Creative Director), Jeffrey Ash, Dori

Berinstein, Roni Selig, Margaret McFeely Golden, Michael Skipper, Gene Korf and Robert Cole; Produced by special arrangement with The Roundabout Theatre Company; Associate Producer: Toby Simkin, Eric Falkenstein and Debbie Bisno.

This production was not part of the Roundabout season that year, nor was it staged in a Roundabout venue. But after The Crucible production at Roundabout Theatres and part of the Roundabout season sometimes did have associate commercial producers.

In 2003 the Roundabout listed Sonia Friedman Productions as an associate producer of *A Day in the Death of Joe Egg,* a revival imported from London's West End. Friedman was one of the two original London producers. In the 2007–8 season Roundabout had multiple associate producers for its mountings of *The 39 Steps* and *Sunday in the Park with George,* both imports from the London stage. *The 39 Steps* was produced in association with Bob Boyett, Harriet Leve / Ron Nicynski, Fiery Angel Ltd., and the Huntington Theatre Company. When it was transferred to a commercial run, additional producers became involved. It's a long list. Bob Boyett's involvement is linked to his long-standing option for the New York transfer of productions that play London's Menier Chocolate Factory Theatre or National Theatre. Harriet Newman Leve and Ron Nicenski have been associate producers with Boyett in recent times. Fiery Angel Ltd. is a London producer that presented the West End commercial run of *The 39 Steps.* Later the Huntington Theatre Company, a U.S. not-for-profit theater, shared the Roundabout production with its audiences The associate producers of *Sunday in the Park with George* were Bob Boyett, Debra Black, Jam Theatricals, Stephanie McClelland, Stewart F. Lane, Bonnie Comley, Barbara Manocherian, Jennifer Manocherian, Ostar Productions, Caro Newling, Neal Street Productions, and Mark Rubinstein.

The IRS first maintained in 1982 that a not-for-profit organization could not function as a general partner in a limited partnership and remain a charitable organization. Not-for-profits can have small for-profit efforts as long as they are insubstantial in size. A typical for-profit effort in a not-for-profit theater might be running a concession stand, selling souvenirs, renting the space for others to use on occasion, and so on.

In the 1982 case *Plumstead Theatre Society v. Commissioner,* the U.S. Tax Court countermanded the IRS, maintaining that not-for-profit organizations could enter into partnerships with commercial entities if the partnership did not create a conflict of interest for the not-for-profit. The court restricted such partnerships to ones where the activity is related to the not-for-profit's stated charitable purpose and where the not-for-profit's resources are not at risk before those of the commercial partners are at risk. The Plumstead Playhouse in Mineola, Long Island, was founded in 1968 by film actors Henry Fonda, Robert Ryan, and Martha Scott and dedicated to reviving classic American plays. Later renamed the Plumstead Theatre Society, the group moved to Los Angeles. In 1978 the group transferred its production of *The First Monday in October* to a Broadway run, produced in association with the Kennedy Center, Washington, D.C. Plumstead is not active now. This ruling enables not-for-profits to enter into some commercial endeavors. The ruling applies not only to theaters; not-for-profit hospitals exploit this finding.

Lincoln Center Theatre

The Lincoln Center Theatre operates the Vivian Beaumont Theatre, a Broadway stage, the Mitzi Newhouse, an off-Broadway house, and it is building a new off-off-Broadway theater that seats ninety-nine. Part of the Lincoln Center for the Performing Arts, the 1960s campus holding the performing spaces for the New York Philharmonic, the Metropolitan Opera, City Opera, and the American Ballet Theatre, the Vivian Beaumont Theatre was one of those strange cases where a theater building was built before there was a not-for-profit theater organization formed to use it. Like many such buildings, the early history of the not-for-profit theaters housed in the Beaumont was highly troubled.

Only in 1985, after years of disuse, was a successful organization formed that revived the Vivian Beaumont Theatre. Lincoln Center Theatre (LCT) was the country's largest not-for-profit theater, but as in 2008, The Roundabout wields a bigger budget. The total budgets for the Kennedy Center and the Center Group in Los Angeles are as large or larger, but those organizations produce and/or present performances in addition to theater. In the latest available IRS filing, LCT's yearly budget was just over $47 million. Personnel costs are low by comparison to most not-for-profit theaters, about 45 percent. About 63 percent of revenues come from ticket sales, more or less average for large not-for-profit theaters. LCT doesn't have subscribers. Instead it offers *memberships.* Members have first access to show tickets, at discount prices. Membership is $50 per year at present. LCT gets about $1.35 million from memberships.

About $21.7 million in the year of reporting, the 2005–6 season, was spent on the extended run of the new musical, *The Light in the Piazza,* which opened in April 2005 and closed July 2006. During the run it grossed $28 million. About $14 million supported the rest of LCT's season: two world premiere plays and one world premiere musical produced in the small theater and two play revivals produced in commercial Broadway houses since *The Light in the Piazza* had an extended run in LCT's large theater. In addition the budget supported developmental workshops and readings, a seminar for training young directors, an education program, and maintenance for its theaters.

LCT filings with the IRS reveal a unique approach to collaborating with commercial entities. Instead of entering into partnerships, the LCT receives loans that are repayable only from net proceeds from the production for which the loan was made. For example, Music Theatre International, a publisher and licenser of musicals, loaned LCT seventy-five thousand dollars towards the recording of the cast album for one show and fifty thousand dollars for another show, both to be paid only from the net profits from the recordings.

More substantially a loan of more than $1.1 million was forgiven and became income in the 2005 season IRS report. The entry is annotated as a "non-recourse loan given to the organization [LCT] to finance part of the production costs of a play in our exempt-purpose program, on condition that the loan would be repayable only from a share of the net operating profit (if any) of this play. When the play closed, the unpaid balance of the loan was forgiven." This loan was probably for the Stephen Sondheim / Nathan Lane adaptation of Aristophanes' *The Frogs,* which closed October 2004; the credits include "Produced in association with Bob Boyett."

Public Animosity, Private Exploitation

Whatever the attitude of the commercial producers toward the greater not-for-profit theater community, animosity for the super-nfps is often expressed around the time of the annual Tony Award nominations. Michael Riedel reported in his "On Broadway" column in the *New York Post,* May 23, 2008, that commercial producers "have long grumbled that the nonprofits get all sorts of breaks, including lower print-ad rates. They also hate to lose out on a Tony, which can boost ticket sales, to institutions that don't live and die at the box office because they're publicly subsidized." The late Gerald Schoenfeld, chairman of the Shubert Organization, liked to say, "There's no profit like nonprofit." Another producer refers to the commercial Broadway theater as the "taxpaying theater" to contrast it with the nontaxpaying not-for-profit theater.

To the charge that the not-for-profit Broadway theaters have advantages over the commercial theater because of tax breaks, charitable giving, and government and corporate grants, Todd Haimes, director of the not-for-profit Roundabout Theatre, responded, "The commercial theater is based on the producer model: You raise $2 million for a show, and if it fails, with the next show you start from zero again. . . . In the nonprofit world, you can't operate like that. If you lose $2 million, you start your next show with a $2 million deficit."

Commercial producers are happy to exploit the not-for-profit theater community to save them money, but Broadway producers are troubled when their shows lose out at Tony Award time to shows mounted by the super-nfps. It's all about money. Yet a sophisticated commercial producer realizes that the productions of the super-nfps help vitalize the brand called Broadway. With so many hugely successful commercial musicals running for years, the esteem and variety of the super-nfps' offerings give Broadway more to crow about. This vitality keeps

Broadway from becoming a sort of adult theme park, populated by phantoms, puppets, squirrelly knights, lions, mermaids, flying nannies, and reworked children's favorites.

The Dance Continues

It was Arena Stage's ambition in 1967 to stage an expensive script—not with hopes of commercial success but because of the importance of the play's themes—that unwittingly started the dance between the not-for-profit and commercial theaters. The not-for-profits' need to exploit all money sources so that they can continue to mount the challenging scripts that play to budget deficits was abundantly fulfilled by the transfer to Broadway of the Public's *A Chorus Line* in 1975. Since then financial pressures, reinforced by tax law and union rules, continue to make the commercial and not-for-profit theaters partners in a complex two-step that is at its best a good thing for both parties.

Afterword

Looking to the Future

As 2009 began, it became clear that the United States and the world were in a recession. Most economists predict this decline will be deep and long. Virtually no individual, organization, or nation can escape the changes resulting from such a macroeconomic event so the theater is changed by it too.

The effect on theater business has already started. In the final months of 2008, many Broadway shows posted closing notices. Several new productions slated to open in the first part of 2009 were postponed; difficulty in financing was usually cited as the cause. Roger S. Berlind, a producer of the 2008 revival of *Gypsy* and other shows, said, "We can't pretend we're immune to the effects of this incredible economic malaise that the country is experiencing. . . . Psychologically, people might feel it's really frivolous to go to theater at $200 a pop."

To the surprise of many, in spring 2009 these newly empty Broadway theaters were snapped up with a surprising number of limited-run, nonmusical plays, many featuring stars from film and television. As a result the 2008–9 Broadway season had more new productions than have been mounted in many seasons. In 2008–9, there were forty-three new productions, 1,548 playing weeks, and $943 million in total revenue. In the previous season, the number of productions was thirty-six, playing weeks were 1,560, and revenue was $983 million. Details of the 2008–9 season are presented in the appendix. This surging crop of plays may actually be connected to the recession. Plays are cheaper to mount than musicals and can recoup their investment in less time. Producers may find it easier to gather investments to mount plays in this market than musicals, although straight plays never make the extraordinary returns that successful, long-running musicals can. The number of Broadway openings in the early months of 2009 have made it look like Broadway is little hurt by this recession, but historically the theater doesn't escape the effects of downturns. During the recessions of both 1972–74 and 1991–93, playing weeks on Broadway dropped below 1,000.

The effects of the recession are being felt in the not-for-profit theater as well. The Tony Award–winning Theatre de la Jeune Lune shuttered because of mounting debt; it put the theater's headquarters in Minneapolis up for sale. When the

Argosy Foundation announced in 2008 it would no longer support Milwaukee Shakespeare, that theater closed. A few of the other not-for-profits shuttered include the Madison Rep in Madison, Wisconsin; the Forum Theatre in Metuchen, New Jersey; the Voodoo Mystere theater in New Orleans; the Foothills Theatre in Worcester, Massachusetts; Jimmy Tingle's Off Broadway in Boston; and the American Musical Theatre of San Jose, California. The *Denver Post* reported in May 2009 that about one-third of Colorado theater companies went dark in 2008. These are probably just the early losses in a series of not-for-profit theaters to close.

The Center Theater Group in Los Angeles is postponing the dark comedy *The Lieutenant of Inishmore* for a year. It's not the only not-for-profit that is changing its programming to respond to the economic crisis. *Backstage East* reports that more not-for-profit theaters are planning coproductions to reduce the costs of sets, costumes, and rehearsals. Other theaters are reducing budgets in the 2009–10 season because of the recession. Shakespeare & Company in Lenox, Massachusetts, cut its budget by $1.1 million. The Oregon Shakespeare Festival trimmed a little more than $2 million from its expenditures. The Guthrie Theater in Minneapolis cut nearly $4 million. Seattle Repertory Theatre's budget went from $10 million to about $6.5 million. In most cases these cuts have resulted in layoffs, unpaid furloughs, and salary reductions.

Theatre Communications Group together with the Theatre Bay Area association conducted a survey of San Francisco–area theaters February through April 2009. The results show that spending in 2009 is projected to decrease by about 4.6 percent. About one-half of respondents expect to have cash-flow problems. In reaction to the recession, at least one-third of theaters responding are doing one or more of the following: adding new ticket discounts, increasing nonticket earnings, and reducing or freezing salaries.

Theater isn't the only performing art experiencing these sorts of losses. Newspapers across the country cite symphony orchestras and dance and opera companies in stress and, in some cases, going under: the Baltimore Opera Company, the Santa Clarita Symphony, and Opera Pacific, to name just three. Cookie Gregory Ruiz, executive director of Ballet Austin, said, "We've seen upturns and downturns but this is pretty extraordinary. . . . It's an economic tsunami." Newspapers are laying off theater and music reviewers, too.

Even the Getty Museum in Los Angeles, famously the richest art institution in the world because of its massive support from the J. Paul Getty Trust, announced in May 2009, that it is slashing its budget by 22 percent and its staff by 14 percent. The value of its portfolio went from $6.4 billion to $4.2 billion in eighteen months.

Michael M. Kaiser, president of the Kennedy Center in Washington and author of *The Art of the Turnaround: Creating and Maintaining Healthy Arts Organizations,* said, "I have never seen a situation like this in my 25 years in the business."

The Kennedy Center started a program in February 2009 called "Arts in Crisis" to counsel troubled arts organizations. By May 2009 some 350 organizations had sought advice. And the center cut its own budget by 6.5 percent

The National Endowment for the Arts published a research note in March 2009 detailing that in the last quarter of calendar 2008 unemployment for all workers grew by 1.9 percentage points, but unemployment for artists climbed 2.4 percent. For actors the unemployment rate in 2007 averaged 23.5 percent and rose to 32.2 percent in 2008.

The cause of this recession is generally agreed to be an economic bubble. A bubble occurs when prices for goods are increased beyond the goods' intrinsic value. The proximate cause for the bursting of this bubble was the discovery that more expensive houses were built than there were qualified people to buy them. When the mortgages started to be foreclosed, other kinds of "irrational exuberance"—to paraphrase former Federal Reserve Board Chairman Alan Greenspan—were laid bare. The deeper cause of the bubble may well have been widely available cheap debt that resulted from the actions of government financial agencies along with lax regulation. Cheap debt encourages buying. When there are many avid buyers, the costs of goods rise. Supply and demand.

When an economy is in a bubble, people feel good. It seems that everyone has money, at least on paper, and most people forget that there is no such thing as a free lunch, that increased returns only come with increased risk. In a bubble people tend to expect continued prosperity, and they rationalize taking higher risks, if they pay any attention at all to the increased risk. This tendency might be seen as a form of hubris, overweening pride that leads to downfall. With risky investments, a small change in the economic climate can have a big impact.

When the bubble bursts, the result is an economic downturn. Just one current fragmentary explanation to support why a bubble is followed by a downturn: all these abandoned homes will stay largely unsold until the economy grows enough that there are qualified buyers for them. With a stockpile of vacant homes, fewer new homes will be built. Thus carpenters will find less work, and suppliers of equipment and matériel for the construction of homes will make fewer sales. The slowdown will decrease the growth of the economy resulting in fewer people becoming financially qualified to buy homes. And this discussion of the housing surplus doesn't start to reckon the impact on the financial markets and so on. This explanation of the causes of the recession is simplistic. In fact it will probably be years before economists have a full understanding of all the causes of this recession. That's often been the case in the past.

It may be that recent years have seen a bubble in the growth of not-for-profit theaters, too. The close of 2008 saw the publication of a study by the National Endowment for the Arts of not-for-profit theaters in the United States. Note that the NEA did not attempt to discern a difference between professional and amateur not-for-profit theaters. As noted earlier, no one has a satisfactory definition of *professional* not-for-profit theater. The NEA study, limited to theaters with budgets of at least seventy-five thousand dollars, found that the number of not-for-profit theaters had doubled between 1990 and 2005. Although the financial state of these theaters looked sound at the time of the survey, the NEA finding about the changing size of the theater audience is troubling. The study found that audience size in this period, measured by a respected national survey of public participation in the arts, did not grow and in some cases declined. The audience for musical theater remained roughly flat as a percentage of the U.S. population, but population growth increased the audience size for musical theater from 32 million in 1992 to 37 million in 2008. The absolute size of the audience for straight plays declined, from 25 million people to 21 million. The question that remains is obvious and stark: how can the number of theaters double if the audience for theater has only increased by 1.7 percent?

This anomaly in the growth of theaters and audiences is why we believe that the not-for-profit theater community is overbuilt and that *consolidation* will come with this recession. As the number of not-for-profit theaters has grown much more than the audience has, consolidation is inevitable. A consolidation happens when the supply of a given good exceeds demand. Weak firms making the product that has the excess supply then merge with other companies, are acquired by larger companies, go into a different line of business, or go under. Eventually supply is balanced with demand, and creation of the given product becomes a viable business once more. There is ample evidence in the nationwide numbers of theater closings that a consolidation of not-for-profit theaters is underway.

A consolidation is emotionally wrenching for all concerned, but the ecology of business demands consolidation when necessary. When a theater closes in a community, the only bright side is that a good part of the earned and unearned income the theater consumed may go to another not-for-profit performing arts organization and the best of the artists freed by the closing will find other, stronger organizations in which to express their talents. More up-to-date information can be found at our Web site, http://www.stagemoney.net.

We believe the theater will find a way to survive in a changed economy not primarily because of the business acumen of the people involved but because of the art of the theater and its eternal importance to the human spirit. Since at least fifth-century B.C.E. Athens, human societies have repeatedly satisfied a need for live performance, a need to come together as a group and be diverted from their cares or enlightened by the social and moral mirror live performance can hold up to a culture.

One recent example of theater's importance to society: in January 2002, less than two months after the deposing of the fundamentalist Taliban regime in Kabul, Afghanistan, the Kabul Theater Company held public performances of its first play since 1995, performances that were welcomed with standing ovations. The Taliban regime outlawed all forms of entertainment; the theater group had continued to work but only at the nearby university that for some unknown reason the Taliban did not censor. The national theater building, built in the 1960s with a revolving stage and seating for seven hundred, was cratered by explosions from the mujahideen civil war of the 1990s, but the performers persevered. The short play, performed in the bombed-out theater, enacted in poetic form the decades of destruction of the Afghan people and culture; it ended with a celebration of a hoped-for return of peace. By 2004 the Kabul Theatre Company toured several Afghanistan provinces and hosted an eight-day theater festival. A sixteen-year-old Afghan woman whose play was performed at the festival said, "Theater can help us find better ways to exist in the future."

Back in the United States and New York City, producer Elizabeth McCann said in 2008, "I don't see any reason to be concerned about the health of Broadway. Even in a good economy, shows fail. It takes a bit of nerve, and people's nerves are jingly now from the stock market. It's always been the survival of the fittest and always will be." Broadway theater, the "fabulous invalid," always goes on somehow. In just the eighty-some years since that sobriquet was first applied, live theater has survived the Great Depression and other recessions; the Second World War and other wars; Senator McCarthy and the House Un-American Activities Committee; waves of immigrants who spoke Yiddish, Spanish, Korean, Arabic, Pashto, and Vietnamese; the great financial and social decline of New York City in the 1970s; and September 11, 2001. There's every reason to believe theater will reinvent its business model once again and survive.

Appendix

2008–2009 Broadway Season Summary

The 2008–2009 season, represented by this table, is not unlike most Broadway seasons in the new millennium. In all, the season grossed close to a billion dollars. Still, this season tells a piece of the story of high risk and return that is Broadway.

Of seventy-seven shows running at some time during the season, ten (13 percent) were "long runs," musicals that opened in an earlier season and/or continued into the next season, running more than five hundred performances, the conventional definition of a long run. Six were "megahit" musicals: *The Lion King*, *The Phantom of the Opera*, *Jersey Boys*, *Mamma Mia!*, *Hairspray*, and *Wicked*. After the close of the season, *Billy Elliot* and the revival of *South Pacific* may be added to the long-running shows. Two nonmusical plays were also long-running, *August: Osage County* and *The 39 Steps*.

Of the seventy-seven shows, twenty-seven (35 percent) made back their investment, twenty (26 percent) did not, and 16 (21 percent) were too-soon-to-tell at the close of the season. Not-for-profits produced 15 shows, about 19 percent.

About 44 percent of the seventy-seven productions—thirty-four shows—were nonmusical plays. An additional four shows, or just over 5 percent, were special or concert shows. A total of eight nonmusical plays originated on Broadway (about 10 percent of all productions).

Of all shows, fifteen (19 percent) were produced by not-for-profit theaters. Another forty-two productions originated in the not-for-profit theater or were imports, mostly from London.

A quick flop, *The Story of My Life* earned less than $265,000, while a hit that opened during this season, *Spring Awakening*, earned nearly $14 million. Even the limited run of *Irving Berlin's White Christmas* earned over $9 million. Feast or famine.

Title	Genre	Season Revenue	Hit, Flop, or NFP‡	New or Revival	Origin	Limited Run
Accent on Youth	Play	$1,351,955	NFP	Revival	NFP	Limited
All My Sons	Play	$11,236,732	Hit	Revival	Bway	Limited
American Buffalo	Play	$739,550	Flop	Revival	Bway	Limited
The American Plan	Play	$2,001,797	NFP	New	NFP	
† August: Osage County	Play	$19,404,187	Hit	New	NFP	
† Avenue Q	Musical	$15,263,915	Hit	New	NFP	
Billy Elliot: The Musical	Musical	$38,014,801	TSTT	New	London	
Blithe Spirit	Play	$762,644	TSTT	Revival	Bway	Limited
* Boeing-Boeing	Play	$12,294,605	Hit	Revival	London	
* Cat on a Hot Tin Roof	Play	$2,881,192	Hit	Revival	Bway	
* A Catered Affair	Musical	$2,816,188	Flop	New	NFP	
* A Chorus Line	Musical	$5,442,714	Hit	Revival	Bway	
Cirque Dreams	Special	$5,166,139	Hit	New	n/a	
* The Country Girl	Play	$2,705,222	Hit	Revival	Bway	Limited
* Cry-Baby	Musical	$1,066,388	Flop	New	NFP	
* Curtains	Musical	$2,244,308	Flop	New	NFP	
Desire Under the Elms	Play	$1,381,950	Flop	Revival	NFP	Limited
Dividing the Estate	Play	$2,796,827	NFP	New	NFP	Limited
Equus	Play	$11,962,266	Flop	Revival	London	Limited
Exit the King	Play	$5,531,534	TSTT	Revival	Australia	Limited
God of Carnage	Play	$9,071,333	Hit	New	France	Limited
* Grease	Musical	$18,245,073	Hit	Revival	Bway	
Guys and Dolls	Musical	$9,231,683	TSTT	Revival	Bway	
* Gypsy	Musical	$22,623,290	Flop	Revival	NFP	
Hair	Musical	$9,817,473	TSTT	Revival	NFP	
* Hairspray	Musical	$18,352,676	Hit	New	NFP	
Hedda Gabler	Play	$2,742,239	NFP	Revival	NFP	Limited
Impressionism	Play	$2,776,559	Flop	New	Bway	Limited
† In the Heights	Musical	$43,483,586	Hit	New	NFP	
Irena's Vow	Play	$2,167,390	TSTT	New	NFP	Limited
Irving Berlin's White Christmas	Musical	$9,354,235	Hit	New	Bway	Limited
† Jersey Boys	Musical	$57,415,967	Hit	New	NFP	
Joe Turner's Come and Gone	Play	$2,195,003	NFP	Revival	NFP	Limited
* Legally Blonde	Musical	$13,773,806	Flop	New	Bway	
* Les Liaisons Dangereuses	Play	$1,613,905	NFP	Revival	NFP	
† The Lion King	Musical	$60,733,819	Hit	New	Bway	
† The Little Mermaid	Musical	$44,067,469	TSTT	New	Bway	
Liza's at the Palace....	Concert	$3,011,648	Hit	New	n/a	
† Mamma Mia!	Musical	$49,167,774	Hit	New	London	
A Man for All Seasons	Play	$3,612,194	NFP	Revival	NFP	Limited
† Mary Poppins	Musical	$40,556,323	Hit	New	London	
Mary Stuart	Play	$2,402,162	TSTT	Revival	London	Limited
next to normal	Musical	$2,440,975	TSTT	New	NFP	
9 to 5	Musical	$5,454,883	TSTT	New	NFP	
The Norman Conquests	Play	$1,663,773	TSTT	Revival	London	Limited
* November	Play	$2,022,146	Flop	New	Bway	
Pal Joey	Musical	$5,574,587	NFP	Revival	NFP	Limited
* Passing Strange	Musical	$1,944,566	Flop	New	NFP	
† The Phantom of the Opera	Musical	$39,976,174	Hit	New	London	
The Philanthropist	Play	$1,439,112	NFP	Revival	London	Limited
Reasons To Be Pretty	Play	$1,513,702	TSTT	New	NFP	Limited
* Rent	Musical	$7,792,969	Hit	New	NFP	
Rock of Ages	Musical	$4,074,186	TSTT	New	Bway	
The Seagull	Play	$6,430,741	Hit	Revival	London	Limited
Shrek The Musical	Musical	$21,776,287	TSTT	New	Bway	
Slava's Snowshow	Special	$1,435,574	Flop	n/a	n/a	Limited
Soul of Shaolin	Special	$1,225,360	Flop	New	China	Limited

(*continued*)

Title	Genre	Season Revenue	Hit, Flop, or NFP‡	New or Revival	Origin	Limited Run
† South Pacific	Musical	$46,730,553	NFP	Revival	NFP	
* Spamalot	Musical	$18,400,000	Hit	New	Bway	
Speed-the-Plow	Play	$8,477,092	Hit	Revival	NFP	Limited
* Spring Awakening	Musical	$13,721,258	Hit	New	NFP	
The Story of My Life	Musical	$264,612	Flop	New	NFP	
* Sunday in the Park with George	Musical	$1,935,525	NFP	New	London	
A Tale of Two Cities	Musical	$4,655,502	Flop	New	NFP	
13	Musical	$4,436,367	Flop	New	NFP	
† The 39 Steps	Play	$11,255,026	NFP/TSTT	New	London	
33 Variations	Play	$4,380,302	Flop	New	NFP	Limited
* Thurgood	Play	$3,130,748	Hit	New	NFP	
[title of show]	Musical	$2,188,131	Flop	New	NFP	
To Be Or Not To Be	Play	$1,166,048	NFP	New	NFP	
* Top Girls	Play	$1,112,934	NFP	New	NFP	Limited
Waiting for Godot	Play	$3,506,959	NFP	Revival	NFP	Limited
West Side Story	Musical	$16,566,072	TSTT	Revival	Bway	
† Wicked	Musical	$75,945,795	Hit	New	Bway	
* Xanadu	Musical	$4,549,824	Flop	New	Bway	
* Young Frankenstein	Musical	$23,800,000 est.	Flop	New	Bway	
You're Welcome America	Play	$6,723,051	Hit	New	Bway	Limited
Total		**$929,191,355**				

Key:

* Show was open as the 2008–9 Season began and closed during that season.
† Show was open as the 2008–9 Season began and remained open at season end.
‡ Based on end-of-season assessment by *Variety: Hit* means show paid back investors. *Flop* means show did not pay back investors. *TSTT* means "too soon to tell;" the show was running but hadn't paid back investors yet *NFP* means the show was not-for-profit; there were no investors.

The three plays of *The Norman Conquest* were capitalized as one show, so it is listed once.

The 39 Steps had a nfp run, followed by a commercial run; which was "too soon to tell."

A one-night fundraiser, *The Yellow Brick Road Not Taken,* was not included.

Selected Bibliography

The most often used, commonly available sources for *Stage Money* are not cited. Articles consulted from the *New York Times, Variety, Back Stage East,* and other widely available periodicals are not enumerated here. Self-descriptions, biographies, or sales figures from individual or organization Web sites are also not cited here. Much specific budget data for not-for-profit theaters came from the IRS 990 forms, which are public records generally available; the IRS sources are omitted from this bibliography. Revenues of Broadway runs came from the Broadway League's Web site, and minimum salaries came from the various unions' Web sites.

What follows is a bibliography of the remaining sources, not mentioned above, used in crafting *Stage Money.*

Adler, Steven. *On Broadway: Art and Commerce on the Great White Way.* Carbondale, Ill.: Southern Illinois University Press, 2004.

"All America's a Stage: Growth and Challenges in the Nonprofit Theatre." Washington, D.C.: National Endowment for the Arts, 2008.

American Theatre Wing. *Working in the Theatre: First and Loudest: The Marketing of Broadway.* Video program in a series. http://americantheatrewing.org/wit/detail/marketing_06_09. Accessed August 10, 2009.

American Theatre Wing. *Working in the Theatre: Off-Broadway Companies.* Video program in a series. http://americantheatrewing.org/wit/detail/off_broadway_companies_01_08. Accessed August 10, 2009.

American Theatre Wing. *Working in the Theatre: Producing Broadway.* Video program in a series. http://americantheatrewing.org/wit/detail/producing_broadway_05_08. Accessed August 10, 2009.

American Theatre Wing. *Working in the Theatre: Producing Commercial Theatre Off-Broadway.* Video program in a series. http://americantheatrewing.org/wit/detail/producing_commercial_theatre_off_broadway_10_06. Accessed August 10, 2009.

American Theatre Wing. *Working in the Theatre: Producing Commercial Theatre.* Video program in a series. http://americantheatrewing.org/wit/detail/producing_commercial_theatre_12_05. Accessed August 10, 2009.

American Theatre Wing. *Working in the Theatre: The Not-for-Profits of Broadway.* Video program in a series. http://americantheatrewing.org/wit/detail/not_for_profits_of_broadway_11_04. Accessed August 10, 2009.

"Artists in a Year of Recession: Impact on Jobs in 2008." Washington, D.C.: National Endowment for the Arts, 2009.

"Artists in the Workforce: 1990–2005." Washington, D.C.: National Endowment for the Arts, 2008.

Bade, Robin, Michael Parkin, and Addison Wesley. *Essential Foundations of Economics.* Upper Saddle River, N.J.: Pearson Education, 2008.

Bartlett, Joseph W. *Fundamentals of Venture Capital.* New York: Madison Books, 1999.

Baumol, William J., and William G. Bowen. *Performing Arts—the Economic Dilemma.* New York: Twentieth Century Fund, 1966.

Benjamin, Gerald A., and Joel Margulis. *The Angel Investor's Handbook.* Princeton: Bloomberg Press, 2001.

Berkowitz, Gerald M. *New Broadways: Theatre across America: Approaching a New Millennium.* New York: Applause, 1997.

Besanko, David and Ronald R. Braeutigam. *Microeconomics,* Hoboken, N.J.: Wiley, 2007.

Blaug, Mark, ed. *The Economics of the Arts.* London: Westview Press, 1976.

Bodie, Zvi, and Alan Marcus. *Essentials of Investments.* New York: McGraw Hill, 2009.

Boroff, Philip. "Big Bucks for Theater Chiefs Draw Criticism as Sign of Excess." http://www .bloomberg.com/apps/ news?pid=20670001. Accessed November 4, 2008.

Bradford, Gigi, Michael Gary, and Glenn Wallach, eds. *The Politics of Culture.* New York: New Press, 2000.

Brooks, C. "Toward a Demand-side Cure for Cost Disease in the Performing Arts." *Journal of Economic Issues* 31 (March 1997): 197–208.

Bryer, Jackson R., and Richard A. Davison. *The Art of the American Musical: Conversations with the Creators.* New Brunswick, N.J.: Rutgers University Press, 2005.

Caltagirone, Christopher. "Critical Capacities in the American Theatre: Interorganizational Relationships between the Commerical and Not-for-Profit Sectors." Report prepared for the Social Theory, Politics and the Arts Conference, George Mason University, 2004.

Cameron, Ben. "The First 40 Years." *American Theatre* (July 2001): 4.

Caves, Richard E. *Creative Industries: Contracts between Art and Commerce.* Cambridge, Mass.: Harvard University Press, 2000.

Cepeda, Ricardo H. Cavazos. "Perceived Quality in Broadway Shows." Preliminary draft, Department of Agriculture and Resource Economics, University of California, Berkeley, undated.

Cherbo, Joni Maya. "Creative Synergy: Commercial and Nonprofit Live Theatre in America." Remarks prepared for the Barnett Arts and Public Policy Symposium, Ohio State University, May 7, 1998.

Chi, Emily C. "Star Quality and Job Security: The Role of the Performers' Unions in Controlling Access to the Acting Profession." *Cardozo Arts & Entertainment Law Journal* (2000): 1–91.

Collins, Tess. *How Theater Managers Manage.* Lanham, Md.: Scarecrow Press, 2003.

Corning, Jonathan, and Armando Levy. "Demand for Live Theater with Market Segmentation and Seasonality." *Journal of Cultural Economics* 26 (Aug 2002): 217–35.

Courty, Pascal. "An Economic Guide to Ticket Pricing in the Entertainment Industry." *Louvain Economic Review* 66, no. 1 (2000): 167–92.

Delle Valle, Anna P. "Is Making Movies All That Different Than Making Plays? Analysis of Cost Structure in Film and Live Theatre." Presented at the 14th Biennial Conference of the Association for Cultural Economics International, Vienna, Austria, July 2006.

Dorbian, Iris. *Great Producers: Visionaries of the American Theater.* New York: Allworth Press, 2008.

Elam, Harry J., Jr., and David Krasner, eds. *African American Performance and Theater History: A Critical Reader.* New York: Oxford University Press, 2001.

Farber, Donald C., and Peter A. Cross, eds. *Entertainment Industry Contracts: Negotiating and Drafting Guide.* Newark, N.J.: LexisNexis, 2007.

Fichera, Dante. *The Insider's Guide to Venture Capital.* Roseville, Calif.: Prima Publishing, 2002.

Fichlander, Zelda. "The Profit in Nonprofit." *American Theatre* 47 (December 2000): 34.

Fields, Anne. "Discount Tickets Star on Broadway." *Stanford Business Magazine* (August 2004). http://www.gsb.edu/news/mbag/smsm0408/research_leslie_consumers.shtml. Accessed September 12, 2009.

Garber, Marjorie. *Patronizing the Arts.* Princeton: Princeton University Press, 2008.

Gates, Henry Louis, Jr. "The Chitlin' Circuit." *New Yorker* 72 (February 3, 1997): 44–55.

Gompers, Paul A., and Josh Lerner. *The Money of Invention: How Venture Capital Creates New Wealth.* Boston: Harvard Business School Press, 2001.

Grippo, Charles. *The Stage Producer's Business and Legal Guide.* New York: Allworth Press, 2002.

Hansmann, Henry B. "The Role of the Nonprofit Enterprise." *Yale Law Journal* 89 (April 1980): 835–901.

———. "Nonprofit Enterprise in the Performing Arts." *Bell Journal of Economics* 12 (Autumn 1981): 341–361.

Happel, Stephen K., and Marianne M. Jennings. "Creating a Futures Market for Major Event Tickets: Problems and Prospects." *Cato Journal* 21 (Winter 2002): 443–52

Headd, Brian. "Redefining Business Success: Distinguishing between Closure and Failure." *Small Business Economics* 21 (2003): 51–61.

Huston, Larry, and Nabil Sakkab. "Connect and Develop: Inside Proctor & Gamble's New Model of Innovation." *Harvard Business Review* 84 (March 2006): 58–67.

Inside Venture Capital. Boston: Harvard Business School Publishing, 2000.

Jarvis, Robert M., et al. *Theater Law: Cases and Materials.* Durham, N.C.: Carolina Academic Press, 2004.

Kaiser, Michael M. *The Art of the Turnaround: Creating and Maintaining Healthy Arts Organizations.* Waltham, Mass.: Brandeis University Press, 2008.

Karp, Larry, and Jeffrey M. Perloff. "When Promoters Like Scalpers." Unpublished paper, December 2004, Department of Agricultural and Resource Economics, University of California, Berkeley. http://repositories.cdlib.org/are_ucb/916R/. Accessed September 12, 2009.

Lane, Stewart F. *Let's Put on a Show! Theatre Production for Novices.* Portsmouth, N.H.: Heinemann, 2007.

Leslie, Phillip. "Price Discrimination in Broadway Theatre." Unpublished paper. http://www.stanford.edu/~pleslie/broadway.pdf.

Long, Robert Emmet, ed. *Producing and the Theatre Business.* New York: Continuum International Publishing Group, 2007.

Lord, Clayton, and Christopher Shuff. "Taking Your Fiscal Pulse: A Report on the Fiscal Health of the San Francisco Bay Area Theatre Community." New York: Theatre Communications Group, 2009.

Lumme, Annareetta, and Colin Mason. "The Returns from Informal Venture Capital Investments: An Exploratory Study." *Journal of Entrepreneurial & Small Business Finance* 5, no. 2 (1996): 139–59.

Maddison, David. "Increasing Returns to Information and the Survival of Broadway Theatre Productions." *Applied Economics Letters* 11 (2004): 639–43.

Marburger, Daniel R. "Optimal Ticket Pricing for Performance Goods." *Managerial and Decision Economics* 18 (August 1997): 375–81.

Markusen, Ann, Sam Gilmore, Amanda Johnson, Titus Levi, and Andrea Martinez. "Crossover: How Artists Build Careers across Commercial, Nonprofit and Community Work." The Arts Economy Initiative Project on Regional and Industrial Economics, Humphrey Institute of Public Affairs, University of Minnesota, October 2006. http://www.haassr .org/html/resources_links/pdf/caCrossover.pdf. Accessed September 9, 2009.

Mason, Colin M., and Richard T. Harrison. "Is It Worth It? The Rates of Return from Informal Venture Capital Investments." *Journal of Business Venturing* 17 (2002): 211–36.

Mayeda, Cynthia. "For Institutions, Is Art the Bottom Line?" *American Theatre* 20 (May–June 2003): 32–39.

McCarthy, Kevin F., Arthur Brooks, Julia Lowell, and Laura Zakaras. "The Performing Arts in a New Era." Santa Monica, Calif.: RAND, 2001.

McCarthy, Kevin F., Elizabeth H. Ondaatje, Laura Zakaras, and Arthur Brooks. "Gifts of the Muse: Reframing the Debate about the Benefits of the Arts." Santa Monica, Calif.: RAND, 2004.

Micocci, Tony. *Booking Performance Tours: Marketing and Acquiring Live Arts and Entertainment.* New York: Allworth Press, 2008.

Moore, Thomas Gale. "The Demand for Broadway Theatre Tickets." *Review of Economics and Statistics* 48 (March 1966): 79–88

———. *The Economics of the American Theatre.* Durham, N.C.: Duke University Press, 1968.

Morris, Valerie B., and David B. Pankratz, eds. *The Arts in a New Millennium: Research and Arts Sector.* Westport, Conn.: Praeger, 2003.

Nygren, Lan Ma, and Jeffrey S. Simonoff. "Bright Lights, Big Dreams: A Case Study of Factors Relating to the Success of Broadway Shows." *Case Studies in Business Industry and Government Statistics* 1 (2007): 1–14.

Ostrower, Francie. "The Diversity of Cultural Participation: Findings from a National Survey." Report for the Urban Institute and the Wallace Foundation, November 2005. http://www.urban.org/UploadedPDF/311251_cultural_participation.pdf. Accessed February 22, 2010.

Parsa, H. G., John T. Self, David Njite, and Tiffany King. "Why Restaurants Fail." *Cornell Hotel and Restaurant Administration Quarterly* 46 (August 2005): 304–13.

Perreault, William, Jr., Joseph Cannon, and E. Jerome McCarthy. *Essentials of Marketing.* New York: McGraw Hill, 2007.

Proscio, Tony, and Clara Miller. "How Steppenwolf Excelled, First on the Boards, Then in the Boardroom, and Ultimately on the Balance Sheet." Report of the Nonprofit Finance Fund, New York, 2003.

Reddy, Srinivas K., Vanitha Swaminathan, and Carol M. Motley. "Exploring the Determinants of Broadway Show Success." *Journal of Marketing Research* 35 (August 1998): 370–83.

Riley, David Franklin. "Ticket Pricing: Concepts, Methods, Practices, and Guidelines for Performing Arts Events." *CultureWork* (January 2002). http://aad.uoregon.edu/culturework/culturework20.html. Accessed September 12, 2009.

Rosen, Sherwin, and Andrew M. Rosenfield. "Ticket Pricing." *Journal of Law and Economics* 40 (October 1997): 351–76.

Rosini, Neil J. and Michael I. Rudell. "Nonprofit Theaters and Subsidiary Rights" Web site of Franklin, Weinrib, Rudell & Vassallo, P.C. December 26, 2008. http://www.fwrv.com/news/article.cfm?id=100796. Accessed September 12, 2009.

Sanders, Michael I. "New Horizons for Nonprofits: How to Structure Joint Ventures with For-Profits." *Business Law Today* (July–August 2000). http://www.abanet.org/buslaw/blt/blt7–sanders.html. Accessed September 12, 2009.

Schaefer, Patricia. "The Seven Pitfalls of Business Failure and How to Avoid Them." Attard Communications, 2006. http://www.businessknowhow.com/startup/businessfailure.htm. Accessed September 12, 2009.

Schiff, Jerald, and Burton Weisbrod. "Competition between For-Profit and Nonprofit Organizations in Commercial Markets." *Annals of Public and Cooperative Economics* 62 (October–December 1991): 619–40.

Schill, Michael H. "The Participation of Charities in Limited Partnerships." *Yale Law Journal* 93 (June 1984): 1375–85.

Shagan, Rena. *Booking & Tour Management for the Performing Arts.* New York: Allworth Press, 2001.

Shapiro, James. *A Year in the Life of William Shakespeare: 1599.* New York: HarperCollins, 2005.

Shuff, Christopher, and Ilana B. Rose. "Taking Your Fiscal Pulse: January 2009." New York: Theatre Communications Group, 2009.

Simonoff, Jeffrey S., and Lan Ma. "An Empirical Study of Factors Relating to the Success of Broadway Shows." *Journal of Business* 76 (2003): 135–50.

Sponberg, Arvid F. *Broadway Talks.* New York: Greenwood Press, 1991.

"Statistical Analysis of Off-Off-Broadway Budgets." New York Innovative Theatre Foundation, April 2008. http://www.nyitawards.com/survey/oobbudgetstudy.pdf. Accessed September 12, 2009.

U.S. Census Bureau. "Performing Arts, Spectator Sports, and Related Industries: 2002." Washington, D.C.: U.S. Department of Commerce, August 2004.

Vogel, Frederic B., and Ben Hodges, eds. *The Commercial Theater Institute Guide to Producing Plays and Musicals.* New York: Applause Theatre and Cinema Books, 2006.

Vogel, Harold L. *Entertainment Industry Economics: A Guide for Financial Analysis,* 7th ed. Cambridge: Cambridge University Press, 2007.

Voss, Zannie Geraud, and Glenn B. Voss with Christopher Shuff and Ilana B. Rose. "Theatre Facts: A Report on Practices and Performance in the American Not-for-profit Theatre

Based on the Annual TCG Fiscal Survey." Published by Theatre Communications Group, New York.

———. "In Whom We Trust IV: Theatre Governing Boards in 2007." Report of the Theatre Communications Group, New York.

Wasser, Daniel M. "Entity Selection for Theatrical Producers: Limited Liability Company or Limited Partnership?" Web site of Franklin, Weinrib, Rudell & Vassallo, P.C. May 12, 2008. http://www.fwrv.com/news/article.cfm?id=100629. Accessed September 12, 2009.

Webb, Duncan M. *Running Theaters: Best Practices for Leaders and Managers.* New York: Allworth Press, 2004.

Wiltbank, Robert. "Investment Practices and Outcomes of Informal Venture Investors." *Venture Capital* 7 (October 2005): 343–57.

Index